GLIMPSES *into* BEELZEBUB'S TALES

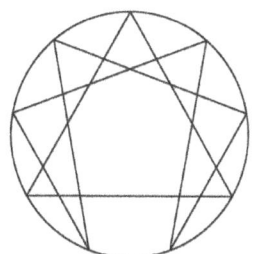

GLIMPSES
into
BEELZEBUB'S TALES

A
COMMONSENSICAL
APPROACH

STEPHEN M. BURZI

Red Elixir
Rhinebeck, New York

Glimpses into Beelzebub's Tales: A Commonsensical Approach ©
copyright 2024 by Stephen M. Burzi

All rights reserved. No part of this book may be used or reproduced in any manner without the consent of the publisher except in critical articles or reviews. Contact the publisher for information.

Paperback ISBN 978-1-960090-48-5
eBook ISBN 978-1-960090-49-2

Library of Congress Control Number 2023923521

Book design by Colin Rolfe

Red Elixir is an imprint of Monkfish Book Publishing Company

Red Elixir
22 East Market Street, Suite 304
Rhinbeck, New York 12572
(845) 876-4861
monkfishpublishing.com

CONTENTS

The First Question: Why?   ix

BOOK ONE

1. The Arousing of Thought   3
2. Introduction: Why Beelzebub Was in Our Solar System   12
3. The Cause of the Delay in the Falling of the Ship Karnak   16
4. The Law of Falling   20
5. The System of Archangel Hariton   22
6. Perpetual Motion   23
7. Becoming Aware of Genuine Being-Duty   25
8. The Impudent Brat Hassein, Beelzebub's Grandson, Dares to Call Men "Slugs"   27
9. The Cause of the Genesis of the Moon   28
10. Why "Men" Are Not Men   30
11. A Piquant Trait of the Peculiar Psyche of Contemporary Man   32
12. The First "Growl"   33
13. Why in Man's Reason Fantasy May Be Perceived as Reality   34
14. The Beginnings of Perspectives Promising Nothing Very Cheerful   35
15. The First Descent of Beelzebub upon the Planet Earth   36
16. The Relative Understanding of Time   38
17. The Arch-absurd: According to the Assertion of Beelzebub, Our Sun Neither Lights nor Heats   40
18. The Arch-preposterous   44

19	Beelzebub's Tales About His Second Descent onto the Planet Earth	47
20	The Third Flight of Beelzebub to the Planet Earth	51
21	The First Visit of Beelzebub to India	53
22	Beelzebub for the First Time in Tibet	55
23	The Fourth Personal Sojourn of Beelzebub on the Planet Earth	58
24	Beelzebub's Flight to the Planet Earth for the Fifth Time	62
25	The Very Saintly Ashiata Shiemash, Sent from Above to the Earth	65
26	The Legominism Concerning the Deliberations of the Very Saintly Ashiata Shiemash Under the Title of "The Terror-of-the-Situation"	67
27	The Organization for Man's Existence Created by the Very Saintly Ashiata Shiemash	69
28	The Chief Culprit in the Destruction of All the Very Saintly Labors of Ashiata Shiemash	71

BOOK TWO

29	The Fruits of Former Civilizations and the Blossoms of the Contemporary	77
30	Art	81
31	The Sixth and Last Sojourn of Beelzebub on the Planet Earth	85
32	Hypnotism	88
33	Beelzebub as Professional Hypnotist	90
34	Russia	91
35	A Change in the Appointed Course of the Falling of the Transspace Ship Karnak	95
36	Just a Wee Bit More About the Germans	96
37	France	97

| 38 | Religion | 100 |
| 39 | The Holy Planet "Purgatory" | 103 |

BOOK THREE

40	Beelzebub Tells How People Learned and Forgot About the Fundamental Cosmic Law of Heptaparaparshinokh	109
41	The Bokharian Dervish Hadji-Asvatz-Troov	111
42	Beelzebub in America	113
43	Beelzebub's Survey of the Process of the Periodic ReciprocalDestruction of Men, or Beelzebub's Opinion of War	118
44	In the Opinion of Beelzebub, Man's Understanding of Justice is for Him in the Objective Sense an Accursed Mirage	122
45	In the Opinion of Beelzebub, Man's Extraction of Electricity from Nature and Its Destruction During Its Use, Is One of the Chief Causes of the Shortening of the Life of Man	124
46	Beelzebub Explains to His Grandson the Significance of the Form and Sequence Which He Chose for Expounding the Information Concerning Man	126
47	The Inevitable Result of Impartial Mentation	128
48	From the Author	129

End Notes   131

THE FIRST QUESTION: WHY?

MANY people with a desire to read George Gurdjieff's opus, *Beelzebub's Tales to His Grandson* may be experiencing more than some difficulty cracking the strange syntax. My aim is to offer a glimpse behind the unfamiliar words and phrasing into the meat of his ideas and exercises.

George Ivanovich Gurdjieff (1866?–1949) was a mystic and spiritual teacher in the first half of the twentieth century. He traveled extensively throughout central Asia, Egypt, Tibet, China, India, the Far East, and southern Russia, studying with various monks, fakirs, and yogis, seeking out the ancient esoteric mysteries of humanity's place and purpose in the universe. After years of almost superhuman efforts, immersing himself in the long-forgotten knowledge of our past, he developed a system of individual evolution called the Fourth Way, which he brought to the Western World. The basic tenant of this system is that we do not yet possess individuality or self-mastery, yet it is our birthright. We have the possibility to awaken to and live from higher states in ourselves and eventually achieve full human potential.

Gurdjieff taught his system for years in many parts of the world; however, circumstances forced him to distill his teaching into ten books in three series under the common title, *All and Everything*. The first series of three books: *Beelzebub's Tales to His Grandson* (additionally titled, *An Objectively Impartial Criticism of the Life of Man*), is probably his most famous—and most difficult to understand—work. His seemingly impenetrable style was intentional because he refused to use "bon ton literary language." *Bon ton* means good manners or form. It's the British ideal of fashionable people in a fashionable society, or the 1960s American equivalent of "beautiful people." We've come to expect this language in everything, because it makes subject matter easy to grasp by using grammatical catchphrases, insider nods, and social winks. Gurdjieff's intention was to derail our typical thinking patterns, force us to question what we're reading, wrestle with the ideas, and come to our own conclusions. Yes, it's a lot of work, because in particular he asks us to examine what comes from the authorities we believe in.

Gurdjieff refused to use the language of the intelligentsia, those who were engaged in shaping the culture of their day. These are the influencers, persuaders, marketers, etc. who gather as many people as possible under their banners by using the language of persuasion. Gurdjieff set out to write in plain language. As ironic as this sounds, he actually wrote in such a way that everyone who reads and digests his books today will get the same message and help.

Gurdjieff had two aims driving his search for wisdom, and they subsequently informed all of his writing. First,

> to understand the exact significance and purpose of the life of man,

and second,

> to discover, at all costs, some manner or means for destroying in people the predilection for suggestibility, which causes them to fall easily under the influence of mass hypnosis.[1]

Beelzebub's Tales to His Grandson presents us with a complete, living, unified, and understandable spiritual whole that is usually hidden from view by our habits of thinking and feeling. His tales provide signposts, maps, hints, and instructions on how to use one's internal compass to further their own spiritual journey. I am persuaded that

THE FIRST QUESTION: WHY?

the book is Divinely inspired: a bible for our modern world, just as the Homeric tales were instructions to the ancient Greeks on how to see and understand the forces creating and maintaining their world. Those stories birthed and nurtured Greece's Golden Age. Likewise, *Beelzebub's Tales to His Grandson* can awaken us to the higher and finer influences always raining down on us, creating and maintaining the world we occupy.

Gurdjieff never explained his ideas, wishing those who were interested in them to struggle on their own to fathom his teachings. Alfred R. Orage (1873–1934) the editor of *The New Age* magazine who helped edit *Beelzebub's Tales*, said that Gurdjieff's task was to write the book, ours is to make the effort to understand it. However, these days we no longer even teach our children how to write by hand, and people communicate using abbreviations, acronyms, and emojis. Because of this literary diet of ours, his combination of language and syntax may be "indigestible" without a little explication.

We live in different times than those of Gurdjieff's life. We have a much thinner skin, and our desire for comfort and pleasure-without-effort has grown exponentially. All of the technological distractions we have and the innumerable labor-saving services we've become dependent on make it almost impossible to spiritually awaken. On top of this, all previously established ways of inner development are crumbling. With few exceptions, people have lost faith in religion, viewing it as one of the causes of the world's distress. Philosophy is a thinking game that leaves the practical side behind, and spiritualism is now a hodgepodge of fantastic beliefs, practices, and rituals revolving around wishful thinking. Gurdjieff offers us a view of the world that makes sense, gives purpose to life, and can be understood with a little extra effort.

With the highest respect for Mr. Orage—who, interestingly, wrote his own commentary on *Beelzebub's Tales*—I'm attempting to provide small toeholds into the breadth and depth of the wisdom that I've discovered in Gurdjieff's tales. His wonderous worldview is for anyone seeking a new hope-filled paradigm to live by. My drive in writing this book sprang from the question, if someone doesn't know a palace awaits them, why would they look for it? So, I wish to reveal some of the beautiful rooms waiting to be visited and a few of the priceless treasures to be found inside them.*

That being said, *Beelzebub's Tales* is not for the dabbler. As the advertisement says, "serious inquires only," because the results are as promised—liberation from the mundane. On the face of the page, the story is an allegory of how the world was created and is maintained, yet if it's only viewed as taking place outside oneself, it's less than useful for the purposes of individual evolution. One idea we must begin to grasp is—As above, so below. Each created cosmos, including humanity and individuals, lives within the larger world above it like a set of Russian nesting dolls where each is a copy of the original on a smaller scale.

Beelzebub's tales were written in accordance with the cosmic laws of three and seven, so they can be read on many levels that reveal deeper and deeper depths of meaning. One of our jobs as a reader is finding the correspondence—in ourselves, our neighbors, and the world at large—to begin to see the organization of the universe and the laws under which it operates. These are the real-life lessons Beelzebub is passing on, but it's up to the reader to verify that's the case.

In his opening chapter Gurdjieff firmly states that all of our knowledge is from suggestibility: What we know someone told us without verification on our part. Our educational system is based on the idea of memorization or learning by rote various facts that certain panels of experts determined were necessary for existence.

---

* Note that in addition to numbered End Notes locators, certain quotations are alternatively followed by parenthetic in-text citations. Passages quoted from *Beelzebub's Tails* are identified by: (BT, page number). These BT quotations are sourced from the following edition: G. Gurdjieff, *All and Everything: Ten Books, in Three Series, of which this is the First Series, Beelzebub's Tales to His Grandson*, (New York: E. P. Dutton, 1964). This edition includes all 1,238 pages of the original 1950 first edition.

THE FIRST QUESTION: WHY?

Though these facts are definitely useful in getting along in life, they're not the limit of knowledge possible for an individual with,

> the boldness to attain the right to be considered by others, and to consider themselves a conscious thinker. (BT, 15)

However, to increase one's consciousness, one's being must also increase, because as St. Mathew says in the King James Bible,

> neither do men put new wine into old bottles: else the bottles break, and the wine runneth out. (Matt. 9:17, KJV)

It makes sense. We're trying to bring forth something that has not existed before—our Sacred Individuality. On this path one's mind, heart, and body will metamorphose into a new being. This also means that what we know (assume) about the worlds inside and outside may not be correct. To truly know, one must verify and then search for the truth if what they were told wasn't the truth.

This takes time, and as Gurdjieff's oft-quoted teacher, the honorable Mulla Nassr Eddin, says, "You cannot jump over your own knees." The process of inner evolution can be sped up, but not rushed. An increase of consciousness requires patience, though that is not a simple achievement. By definition, patience is connected to forbearance, the ability to endure with forgiveness,

> letting go of negative emotions such as vengefulness, and an ability to have mercy towards and wish the offender well.[2]

The word mercy comes from a French expression meaning the price was paid, and the debt canceled or forgiven. In the context of *Beelzebub's Tales*, first, we need to have mercy for the author. He is intentionally pushing our buttons to get us out of our comfort zones—the only way to generate the heat needed to change. When we're uncomfortable, instead of getting negative we can use the agitation to further our wish to evolve. So, we also need to have mercy on ourselves for the frustration, pique, and annoyance that comes along with a good spiritual prodding.

Some say that *Beelzebub's Tales to His Grandson* was written only for students of Gurdjieff's work. I had the book long before discovering the Fourth Way and continued reading it long after on my own. So, after more than forty years of study I can say with surety that the book was written for all those who have ears to hear and want to know the way out of the prison of life as described in the story of Plato's cave. For those readers, I've highlighted certain ideas in each chapter as ways to loosen the chains binding us to our current worldview.

If one follows Gurdjieff's friendly advice to read his book three times, it will begin to have the effect he wishes for us—diminishing our imaginary selves and beginning a spiritual rebirth of our real selves. According to his teaching, reading three times is reading from three of our centers or brains. When we read the book like a newspaper, scanning a page, picking out words and phrases—this is done from the *moving center*. Reading out loud involves our *emotional center* because—as we listen to the sound, tone, and inflection of our voice—it elicits an emotional response. And lastly, we're asked to apply our *intellectual function* to wrestle with these ideas and get the gist of his meaning. In other words, to get the full benefit from his writing that Gurdjieff wishes for us, we must dive into the reading with all of our being.

If we follow Gurdjieff's advice, *Beelzebub's Tales to His Grandson* works a sort of esoteric magic, and we may discover that the mansion is waiting to be occupied, and ways to do that.

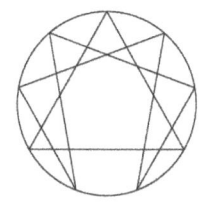

BOOK ONE

CHAPTER ONE

THE AROUSING *of* THOUGHT

GURDJIEFF begins with a prayer, aligning himself from the top down as he's about to embark on this new journey of writing. Proper alignment is the beginning of any spiritual journey. We must at some point answer the question: What do I wish to attain for myself, my neighbor/family, and my God on this journey? We need an aim to get anywhere.

Gurdjieff pronounces his prayer, "not only aloud, but even very distinctly and ... with a wholly-manifested-intonation" (BT, 3). This means that he's praying from his mind, heart, body, soul, spirit, I, essence, conscience, and consciousness together.

At present we're life-driven with little awareness or choice, like the shiny ball in the pinball machine. People assume they're a unified being because they see the same face in the mirror each morning. However, very few people are inwardly self-directed, and intentionally striving for their aims and wishes. Mostly people feel like victims, trapped by the circumstances of their life. Gurdjieff's teaching is aimed at increasing consciousness, developing being, and creating individuality.

Gurdjieff makes no promises about your journey's outcome because you cannot work for results. It just doesn't work. Instead, he's teaching a method of investigation and exploration into the unknown of ourselves and the universe, with the hope that we'll discover our unique place and purpose in life as he provides the tools necessary to achieve it.

As such, Gurdjieff will not write,

just anything "so-so," as for instance, something of the kind for reading oneself to sleep, but weighty and bulky tomes. (BT, 4)

(As you read Beelzebub's tales, keep in mind Gurdjieff's sense of humor.)

* * *

Gurdjieff tells us that these days anyone with free time, if their rent is paid, typically falls ill with the urge to write something. This is proven by the millions of books put out on the market every year by traditional publishing companies, e-books, self-publishers, books-on-demand, vanity presses, printers, and others. However, most of what's out there is written from self-aggrandizement, the need to develop a following. Today, the need for a following is a particularly virulent craze, and as in olden times there are those who are more than willing to shame or embarrass themselves to pay for their fifteen minutes of adulation.

Typically, authors zoom in on a particular detail to explain various theories of how the world works. The problem is that they only have pieces of the picture. On the other hand, Gurdjieff's universe is whole and interconnected, and can organically lead one to their life's true purpose.

Though Gurdjieff had no wish to write, circumstances forced his hand. He had a near fatal car accident, and with it a realization that his work for the sake of future generations couldn't continue on its own without his guidance. He had to find a way to ensure that his teaching survived his passing. So, Gurdjieff distilled not only his ideas, but his methods into ten books in such a way that every reader will have to confront themselves as they confront the material.

* * *

This opening chapter is like the prologue of a symphony or an opera where Gurdjieff outlines the ideas he'll investigate during the course of his tales. At the same time, he issues a warning to the reader that continuing on into his book will cause:

> most [to] lose the "wealth" they have, which was either handed down to them by inheritance or obtained by their own labor, in the form of quieting notions evoking only naïve dreams, and also beautiful representations of their lives at present as well as their prospects in the future. (BT, 5)

This is a painful look at life, filled with the hopes of winning the lottery, finding the perfect mate, living in a dream home with the children of our choice or without them, and going to heaven when we're done. We hang onto these dreams until death closes in and we look back, wondering where all the time went. "If only" are the saddest words one can speak at the end of their life.

Gurdjieff called the modern condition "waking sleep," and his system was a way to awaken to our real lives and wishes. In our present state of our almost magical sleep, we're unaware of other possibilities as we watch our lives pass us by. Gurdjieff's wish is that while we still have time to change, we make the effort to awaken to our true natures. This is a difficult idea to grasp because we believe that we already possess consciousness, individuality, unity, and self-mastery. When asked, we say, "Why, of course I'm awake. I'm here talking to you, aren't I?" However, a deeper look proves this is not the case. If we're sincere with ourselves, we often say and do things that bring us befuddlement or regret.

> For the good that I would, I do not: but the evil which I would not, that I do.[3]

We can see this idea in operation when we ask ourselves things like, "Why did I say that to them?" "Why didn't I do that just now?"

"How did I get into this situation?" *Beelzebub's Tales* can help us discover the why and how, and show us the way to overcome this anomaly in our beings. First, we must learn how our thinking function works.

Gurdjieff says that there are two kinds of mentation, roughly translated as thinking-perceiving. *Mentation by thought* employs "words, always possessing a relative sense." This is the intellectual process of choosing the best word to express our meaning by our grasp of its dictionary definition. This data has accumulated in us mechanically throughout our lives, like all the trivia that we know. By the time we leave grade school (kindergarten, some say) we've developed an inner attitude that says we know all that we need to in order to deal with life. Yet, this attitude relies on habits of thinking and feeling implanted in us by parents, relatives, friends, teachers, and life in general.

Mentation by form "proper to all animals as well as to man," is based on the accumulated knowledge of our past experiences. It's dependent

> upon the conditions of geographical locality, climate, time, and, in general, upon the whole environment in which the arising of the given man has proceeded. (BT, 16)

For instance, bread is a universal concept. Yet everyone has a different experience of bread. To some it means: bleached, white, factory-made—to others: handmade organic whole grain, flat bread, sourdough, buns, rolls, baguettes, challah, pita, wraps, and so on. This is an individual's definition of bread based on life experience.

See the problem? When someone says the word *bread*, everyone is sure they know what is being discussed, yet everyone has a different idea in mind. It's the same with all words: *man, woman, spirit, soul, evolution,* etc.; so, imagine the confusion a simple discussion can cause without people realizing. This is what the Bible refers to as the Tower of Babel, or the confusion of tongues.

These two types of mentation are central to the story of the Transcaucasion Kurd. He thinks he knows what a fruit should taste like because he's familiar with fruit, and after all, he's at a fruiter's shop. Therefore, using mentation by form, he assumes the shiny red-pepper pods should taste sweet and delicious because they look like the other "fruits" he's eaten. It is only when the definition of fruit is applied (mentation by thought) do we realize a fruit is simply the part of the plant that develops from a flower and contains seeds. Examples are pumpkins, cucumbers, pea pods, beans, grains, nuts, corn, olives, squash, and tomatoes. Although most of these have a kind of sweetness to them, they're not like apples, plums, nectarines, pears, and so on—which are sweet by their definitions.

It is the same with Gurdjieff's writing, we can't assume we know what he's saying because certain words or expressions are familiar. We must perform due diligence and apply both types of mentation to get the meaning of these ideas.

* * *

Gurdjieff tells us that he's experimentally proven that there are two different consciousnesses in people. One he calls our daily consciousness—filled with life knowledge, which is

> the perception of all kinds of accidental, or on the part of others intentionally produced, mechanical impressions.
> (BT, 25)

Little effort is required beyond memorization to attain this knowledge. In fact, we are fed this kind of knowledge throughout our lives from everyone we meet, including all the various forms of modern technology. This is the knowledge that we're expected to act from in life. On the other hand, our subconscious consists of what has been passed on to us from generation to generation through our bloodlines, that's "rubbed up" against our daily life experiences. This is education in the school of hard knocks. So, our subconscious is the result of the efforts we make to turn hard-earned knowledge into the "fire is hot, do not touch" understanding we need in order to evolve.

As such, it can be said that our subconsciousness is the seat of our understanding because it's where our knowledge and being (accumulated experience) join together. Gurdjieff teaches that our subconscious is our real consciousness because conscience, which is our connection to the Divine, resides there. This is why we can occasionally experience the resolution of a difficult problem or the clarification of a troubling situation in our dreams, which can come from our subconscious. This is not to imply that all dreams are insightful, useful, or worth paying attention to. Many are simply the shedding of the waste of mental function.

* * *

Gurdjieff gives three injunctions to anyone serious about inner development. The first is to never do as others do, which came to him as a commandment from his grandmother. One cannot create individuality by following another's way. We must insist on making our own choices and learning from them. This is what separates Gurdjieff's teaching from other studies of enlightenment, because the others typically require that one give the responsibility for their lives over to the guru or teacher. Beelzebub's tales never tell us what to do, although they advise against doing certain things we'd be better off not doing. They show us a world similar to our own but filled with adults who are all in one degree or another working for the benefit of future generations, which is an indicator of higher levels of consciousness and reason.

Also, if we follow another's way, we could end up like the devout man standing at the pearly gates. When St. Peter asked him what he did in life to deserve entrance into heaven, he replied with humility that he lived his life striving to be like Moses. Shockingly, St. Peter turned him away, saying, "We already have a Moses."

The second injunction is to question everything; take nothing for granted. The story about Gurdjieff's tooth being knocked out exemplifies this idea. This strange tooth

> had seven shoots and at the end of each of them stood out in relief a drop of blood, and through each separate drop there shone clearly and definitely one of the seven aspects of the manifestation of the white ray. (BT, 33)

He showed this fantastic tooth to the local barber surgeon, "a specialist in extracting teeth." After a casual glance he said it was nothing special, just a wisdom tooth, which everyone had. This is life's typical response to the miraculous, and these are the kind of "facts" we've been told all our lives. To see the miraculous for ourselves we must question what we know, and those we take for authorities. Position in society doesn't equal level of understanding. This is one of the problems with our world—the best people are not in charge. Knowing that everyone makes mistakes means all facts must be verified to be useful in the search for enlightenment.

Gurdjieff's third injunction, "If you go on a spree then go the whole hog including the postage," is an "all universal principle of living" that is almost self-explanatory. When striving to make an aim or going for your wish, don't scrimp; go all the way, and be willing to pay any extra unforeseen expense. First, it'll prepare you for unexpected circumstances that are law conformably bound to arise. Second, it'll help you stay positive when you encounter them. Most of us give up five minutes too soon, or cut corners, or refuse to pay an extra cost, or make an extra effort necessary to reach completion. That's why we keep circling around the same issues.

Gurdjieff takes this last injunction to heart in his writing because his story is not just about the Earth, and his hero isn't just any "Tom, Dick, or Harry." He's writing on a universal scale, by which he means on one appropriate to each different level, including ours. In terms of the story's breadth, he begins shortly after the beginning of creation, that moment science thinks of as the big bang. Taken internally, he's telling our individual stories from the moment of conception.

* * *

Gurdjieff picks Beelzebub for his hero, knowing this choice will agitate the reader from the title onward, as if "blinded flies" were buzzing around in their heads. Agitation is necessary to arouse us out of our passive intellectual and emotional slumber. A question to keep alive while reading is what do all these beings and situations represent internally?

For instance, he also chooses the Devil because of his curly tail. As Gurdjieff says, curls are never natural but always due to some manipulation, (i.e., vanity). So, he will appeal to this feature, understanding that if he flatters the Devil with the title of hero, he will do all in his considerable power to help see that these tales become popular. If we wish to make an aim in this world, we must learn about the different features in us and how to find the right ones to tickle that will aid our aim, and disregard the rest.

Jesus Christ said something similar to his disciples about how to get along in the world:

> Behold, I send you forth as sheep in the midst of wolves:
> be ye therefore wise as serpents, and harmless as doves.
> (Matt. 10:16, KJV)

There is no place for naïveté or willful ignorance on the road to inner development. We must know the ways of the world in order not to be stymied by them, and have them serve our aims.

* * *

Gurdjieff knows his tales will be poking a sleeping dragon in us, but he is not worried. Like the Karapet of Tiflis, he's learned the secret of warding off negativity directed toward him from others, something all of us must learn in our struggle to evolve. The path to individual evolution goes against the flow of life, and as the old saying goes, anyone who stands up in life will be hammered down, bent over, or pulled out. Think about children continuously asking "Why?" At some point something in us just wants them to be quiet and stop bothering us. The child eventually gets put to sleep by these attitudes. It takes an effort to raise a child whose mind, heart, and body remain open and active to higher influences. This applies to raising the inner child as well.

* * *

The last thing I'd like to point out in his opening chapter is how Gurdjieff signs the book, because as he says, "I must in any case in respect of my own signature, be very, very careful." The Fourth Way teaches that there are seven levels of men and women, corresponding to the seven levels of the universe. Most of us fall into the first three categories, which are the mechanical levels of life. Beyond these there are increasingly higher levels of consciousness, and usefulness until one becomes a permanently unified, inwardly directed, individual being—a unique braincell in the mind of God.

Gurdjieff has signed *Beelzebub's Tales to His Grandson* with seven names. I've read this book many more than three times, yet this is still a shock to me. I can feel something inside wanting to put Gurdjieff on my own level. Yes, of course much smarter than me, but basically, he's just another guy like so many others I've read in my life. However, the question this raises cannot be answered as a matter of faith. Gurdjieff does not wish to be put on a pedestal, nor does he want followers singing his praises. He'd prefer workmates among the people who wish to learn what he's discovered. This is why his seventh name is simply a "Teacher of Dancing."

CHAPTER TWO

INTRODUCTION: WHY BEELZEBUB WAS *in* OUR SOLAR SYSTEM

THIS chapter establishes the time-scale of Gurdjieff's story. In our time it's 1921. On the scale of the Megalocosmos it's 223 years after creation was initiated. Considering that Earth is estimated to be over 4.5 billion years old, what is this cosmic scale of time? The exact number is not as important as the idea that different levels of the universe have different times. Take for example the world of a common mayfly, which is born, matures, mates, procreates, grows old, and dies; living the equivalent of our eighty-year life in about twenty-four hours—for us, one day.

Further along the scale we can take Nature all together. Her trees and foliage exhale oxygen during the day and inhale it at night. If we call this one full breath in 24 hours, and if we calculate an average of 23,040 breaths a day for us, Nature's day is about 63 of our years long. Subsequently, its equivalent life span is about 2.5 million years long. Carrying this ratio out to the farthest end of the scale the life of the Megalocosmos, the dwelling place of His Endlessness, can be calculated to 9^{1028} years old, which is just over one octillion or a billion, billion, billion years.[4]

The Nature we know is estimated to be about 3.5 billion years old, making humanity a very late comer into the universe, and situated farthest from its initial creative impulse. This is quite the reverse of how we perceive ourselves and our place in the world—i.e., "God saved the best for last."

The apparent discrepancy in the estimations of Nature's life span is that there have been five ages of Nature on the planet or five generations, each slightly overlapping the other. The first was the Archean age, when only microbes lived, after which came the Proterozoic age, during which the earliest fungi developed. This was followed by the Phanerozoic age, which contained the first true vertebrates; and then came the Mesozoic era, the age of the dinosaurs. Mankind only appeared at the beginning of the last age, called the Cenozoic. Each period is one in which Nature was born, matured, and died to an old way of life—and was reborn to a new one.

Scale and relativity are everything.

* * *

Beelzebub was initially called to serve on His Endlessness' dwelling place for his "extraordinarily resourceful intelligence." But at that time, he was still an "impetuous youth," and when he saw something he thought illogical in the running of the Megalocosmos, he stuck his nose in where it didn't belong.

Because of his persuasiveness and high standing among his fellow angels, his questioning spread and practically brought heaven to the brink of revolution. The Lord God put a stop to the upheaval and subsequently exiled Beelzebub. So far, this story parallels the Christian account as told by the English poet John Milton (1608–1674) in his epic poem Paradise Lost, considered one of the greatest works of English literature. It was Milton who penned Satan's infamously prideful words, "Better to reign in hell than serve in heaven."[5]

Milton tells us God banished the Devil to the farthest reaches of the universe as punishment for his transgression. In *Beelzebub's Tales*, that place is our solar system, on our galaxy's outer edge. This is a blow to self-importance, but thinking logically about our solar system's creation from the center out, the way all life unfolds, we are farthest away from the life-giving core.

After this, Gurdjieff's tale diverges from Milton's account because he tells us that Beelzebub's youthful transgression has been pardoned by the Almighty Creator of All. This was partly due to help he gave to a certain Sacred Individual regarding ending the practice of animal sacrifice on Earth, and from the humble and helpful way he's lived since his exile. Beelzebub's tale is one of sin, expulsion, and redemption that reveals something significant about the nature of Divinity.

In a different book, Gurdjieff asks the following questions:

> Why should He, being as He is, send away from Himself one of His nearest, by Him animated, beloved sons, only for the "way of pride" proper to any young and still incompletely formed individual, and bestow upon him a force equal but opposite to His own?[6]

He comes to understand that the separation of the Devil from the Divine is an intentional sacrifice on the part of Divinity, the purpose of which is to create a reminding factor that will evoke a striving for unity. In other words, separation is the first step of the creative process. "God divided the light from the darkness."[7] In emotional language, He created a longing for reunion.

* * *

The reason Beelzebub is relating these tales is because he's taken on the sacred duty of educating his grandson Hassein about the laws of world creation and world maintenance. This knowledge is indispensable for spiritual development because it shows us the place we occupy in creation, our purpose for being here, and how to achieve those higher states as a station.

Beelzebub has made his new home on Mars, named after the ancient Greek God of struggle. One of the first tasks he sets for himself is to build a large observatory to investigate "the conditions of the existence of beings" in the worlds surrounding him. This is also a metaphor for the Fourth Way practice of self-observation, which is done on three levels: impartially observing oneself, one's neighbor, and the world in general. That way, when we see something onerous in ourselves, we can also see it in others and in the world at large, making the feature less personal and more possible to separate from and eventually overcome.

* * *

The spaceship's name is Karnak. It means chamber of the heart in Sanskrit. So, it's necessary to be in an emotional place to take in these ideas. Also, all of the discussions between Beelzebub, his grandson, and his faithful and ever-present servant Ahoon take place under the "glass bell" of the ship. Internally, one meaning of this is that the higher self, lower self, and essential self are gathered together under one's pineal gland, which the French mathematician and philosopher, René Descartes (1596–1650) called "the principal seat of the soul and the place in which all our thoughts are formed."

Many ancient traditions called this gland "the third eye" because, when active, it becomes a channel between the physical and spiritual worlds. In a newborn baby the pineal gland is open to the heavens, and the child is filled with the higher influences raining down. This is one reason for a pregnant woman's glow, because those influences are also filling her. After birth the baby's skull slowly thickens and that connection is lost until, as an adult, they can make the effort to reopen the link.

CHAPTER THREE

THE CAUSE *of the* DELAY *in the* FALLING *of the* SHIP KARNAK

One point of this chapter is to show the Megalocosmos as an organized, unified whole with a single purpose (except the peculiar men-beings of the Earth). His Endlessness' body or dwelling place requires maintenance and new creations for its health and well-being, just like our bodies. Gurdjieff's worldview is that all of creation has a part to play in this highest cosmos, and there is work to do and jobs to be filled at every level. We can appreciate the analogy of the captain of the spaceship *Karnak*, who started out as a sweeper about the time Beelzebub was exiled and has now worked his way up the ranks, taking on more responsibility as his father before him, who now rules over a solar system.

This is not our typical idea of an afterlife—be good for eighty or so years and then go to heaven, where you'll float around eating honey, drinking milk, and singing God's praises. Gurdjieff shows us a world where we were created with a higher purpose. This is an important idea to grasp. If your world view is a universe full of pieces of rock and balls of gas flying through space, and that there's eighty years of this life and then an eternity of the next—you might as well put the book down now. However, if this idea of levels of usefulness makes sense, it allows one to see the many possibilities of individual evolution in this life and the next.

* * *

We're all working for Divine purposes either consciously or unconsciously, as in the present case where Beelzebub is doing his duty, suffering the vicissitudes of a long journey on his very old planetary body to attend a conference on important cosmic matters. On the way, the captain needs Beelzebub's advice because there's a dangerous situation ahead, and he doesn't know whether to wait it out or try to maneuver around it. How familiar is this event? We even have a name for it—between a rock and a hard place. The answer is from a wise saying of his highly respected teacher, Mullah Nassr Eddin, which brings in a third choice:

> When an event is impending which arises from forces immeasurably greater than our own, one must submit. ... We will pass the time of our unavoidable delay in conversation useful to us all. (BT, 57)

This is a very different attitude from our typical approach to life—going through it at hyper speed, trying to get everything we're supposed to. Our lives aren't ordered from the top down, which is one of the reasons why we avoid bad situations or bully our way through them, beating our heads against a problem or multitasking ourselves into oblivion. We don't have a right relationship to time—the time of our lives. A question to constantly ask is, "How do I get the maximum spiritual profit from this moment?"

Hassein, who partly represents the childlike nature of us all, is thrilled at this prospect of a delay, because

> the talks of my dear grandfather always bring out tales of places where he has been, and you know also how delightfully he tells them and how much new and interesting information becomes crystalized in our presences from these tales. (BT, 57)

This is an extremely different attitude from today's view of the elderly. In our obsession with youth, we think the usefulness of a person diminishes with their age. It's the essence of superficiality because experience is the best teacher.

* * *

From a common-sense point of view, why wouldn't the first cosmos, the highest cosmos, be organized under higher principles and work under higher cosmic laws? What do we think the dwelling place of His Endlessness looks like? If as above—so below is true, then each higher level of the universe would be similar to our own (minus the pollution) except many times more beautiful, subtle, and sublime. And from the opposite view, even at the very highest levels of creation, there's necessary work to do.

Another question to wonder about is why we believe we're alone in the universe? This idea is not based on any kind of science or religious belief but is held in place by self-importance. Humanity is opposed to thinking they're only a small part of a greater whole because it might turn out that it's not fulfilling its purpose. This is also why we still believe that Earth was made for mankind's private use, and treat it accordingly.

* * *

One of the most intriguing sections of this chapter is when Beelzebub tells Hussein about the different beings living on the various planets in our solar system—in particular the beings on the moon. He says,

> there is still another planet, quite a small one, bearing the name Moon, in that solar system, my dear boy. Though the beings of this planet have very frail "planetary bodies," they have, on the other hand, a very "strong spirit," owing to which they possess extraordinary perseverance and capacity for work. I happened to notice that during two of our years they "tunneled," so to say, the whole of their planet . . . where they are protected from all the

vagaries of the mad climate inharmoniously changing the state of the atmosphere. (BT, 62)

Although this tale is certainly allegorical—after all, we've been to the moon and didn't find any signs of life yet. However,

at the close of the Apollo age in 1972, a year before the final moonwalk, a NASA researcher argued that vast tunnels [must] lie beneath the lunar surface, ... but the lava [?] tunnels of the moon, like the mythical canals of Mars, proved elusive.[8]

Then in 2009, almost sixty years after the publication of *Beelzebub's Tales*, Japanese scientists with the assistance of two NASA satellites discovered "a 50-kilometer long, 100-meter-wide cavern on the moon."[9] To date, over two hundred such tunnels that are classified as lava tubes have been charted on the moon, and several space agencies have proposed exploring them by various means, including using lunar rovers.

Numerous governments with aspirations for lunar colonies are looking at adapting this cavern, and other similar tunnels as suitable base stations for human habitation, citing that they would require only minimal additional work to protect people from the dangerous atmospheric conditions on the lunar surface, such as extreme temperature swings varying from +266 °F to -292 °F in a day-night cycle, mega dust storms, hazardous radiations, and micro-meteoritic impacts.

So, was this a guess Gurdjieff made about the structure of the moon, ancient knowledge he uncovered—or something else?

CHAPTER FOUR

THE LAW *of* FALLING

It's easy to assume that the points of stability are the centers of gravity of the celestial bodies. However, gravity loses its effect over distance, a phenomenon experienced as weightlessness. So, what is the law of falling? One way to think about it is attraction. Most of us have felt this force, particularly when we see someone across a crowded space and are immediately drawn to them, or conversely repulsed by them. This force is partly made up of what is called Elekilpomagtistzen, which can be loosely translated as electromagnetism. We have these same forces in us, and they go on to form our atmosphere or aura, as it's sometimes referred to.

This was also the force used by Saint Venoma to obliterate any air, gas, or fog surrounding a celestial body in order to take full advantage of the law of falling. What might this mean internally? One meaning is that our personal atmosphere can, so to speak, clear a way for us in life. We've all seen people with that 'stay away from me' vibe, and probably had that look on our own faces once or twice. Then there are those we're instinctively drawn to for some unknown reason, without a word being said. Likewise, our electromagnetic aura can eliminate other's vibrations coming toward us by using our accumulated force, allowing us to not identify with them. We must learn how to separate our real selves from our "life selves"—so that when life sends out its siren call, trying to draw us to something, we're not forced to listen.

Another idea behind "points of stability" is that influences eventually fall to the lowest point in us, like the expression "familiarity breeds contempt." So, this is a warning of sorts to nourish and care for the understanding growing inside us, because our work must be cumulative like storing Elekilpomagtistzen in a battery, and kept under our control in order to successfully traverse the spaces outside and inside ourselves.

* * *

One way to look at these trans-space ships is as schools of inner development, and their ways of locomotion are different ways of working on oneself in that type of school. The earlier models required completely empty space for locomotion, like the remote monasteries Gurdjieff visited. These monks completely separated themselves from life in order to achieve inner peace, like their European counterparts who also give up the temptations of life to achieve closeness to Jesus Christ. Though this way is effective, it's cumbersome, requiring numerous manipulations and tremendous accumulated energy. That meant that a student could only move if the entire school moved.

CHAPTER FIVE

THE SYSTEM *of* ARCHANGEL HARITON

THIS marvelous new system of propulsion uses an ingenious invention—a special hermetically sealed barrel with a hinged lid that fills with dense matters and expands them, exerting pressure on a lever like any steam, diesel, gasoline, or rocket-powered engine—transforming fuel into motion.

The atmosphere surrounding planets is similar to the vibe we put off, made up of our different energies—electrical, chemical, mental, magnetic, cosmic, etc.—mixed with the heavier matters of negative thoughts and feelings we may be having. The new system is a metaphor for working on oneself in the system that Gurdjieff called the Fourth Way, combining the three traditional ways of the Fakir, the Yogi, and the Monk in such a way as to increase their simplicity and speed of working.

This new system is based on taking in the negative matter of our lives and using it to fuel our inner evolution—transforming our negative emotions into positive emotions. This includes learning how to bear the unpleasant manifestations of others, a parallel idea to Christ's teaching to love one's enemies, which is as much for the Divine's well-being as it is for our enemy's and ours.

CHAPTER SIX

PERPETUAL MOTION

One thing Gurdjieff got wrong in this chapter is that the search for perpetual motion wasn't short lived. You can watch any number of videos, made as late as 2023, proving or disproving the possibility of building a device to run forever without needing an additional outside energy input, (i.e., it runs on gravity). This wishful thinking is deeply ingrained in us, resulting from the desire to get something for nothing. Internally this translates into wanting to evolve without any effort. It's that same desire that drives us to seek magic pills to lose weight and seduces us into participating in various forms of virtual reality—excitement without effort. We're tramps and lunatics with imaginary values, imaginary interests, and imaginary possibilities.

Oddly, a waterwheel, which substitutes the flow of water for the force of gravity, will "work perpetually without needing the expenditure of any outside materials" until the river dries up. But I digress. Gurdjieff is teaching about the way toward inner evolution through common sense, which requires a willingness to make extra efforts over and above life's requirements.

* * *

Knowing Gurdjieff's fondness for hiding secrets within the simplest sentences, I researched some of the different materials used in the "barrel's" construction.

- Amber is a good insulator because it's a poor conductor. Ancient cultures believed it to be petrified sunlight and used

it as a talisman for courage and self-confidence and a symbol of wisdom and endurance.
- Platinum is one of the rarest and least reactive metals on Earth, with very high malleability and corrosion resistance. It's used spiritually to align the physical body with the ethereal.
- Anthracite coal can have a carbon content as high as 98 percent and, when burned as a fuel, produces an almost smokeless fire. Spiritually, it is called "the stone of remorse," allowing the forces of understanding and acceptance to penetrate into oneself.
- Copper is a malleable metal that's both electrically and thermally conductive. It's also necessary for the health of a human being, as it helps create red blood cells and certain energy needed for the body. Spiritually, copper is the giver of positivity.
- Ivory is prized for making air-tight containers. Spiritually it's associated with purity, innocence, and Divinity. The color also stands for hope and new beginnings.
- Finally, today, mastic is commonly associated with a sealer to fill joints. However, organic mastic was first used as a food stuff, which is where the English word *masticate* (to chew) comes from. Chewing mastic improves digestion, the liver, and oral health. Also, it can be burned as an incense to help with mental clarity, energize the body, and dispel sadness.

So, developing those traits—courage, wisdom, endurance, a thick-though-flexible skin, self-confidence, corrosion resistance to the negativity of life, proper alignment with higher worlds, purity of heart, remorse for past unbecoming deeds, and mental clarity—spiritually transforms us into finer and more useful beings.

CHAPTER SEVEN

BECOMING AWARE *of* GENUINE BEING-DUTY

When Hassein is struck by the realization that "everything was not born with [him] like his nose," he asks what he owes for all the intense work different beings have done to bring it about. Few of us ever ask this question. Mostly we're in an opposite state of mind, wondering how to get what *we're* owed or entitled to, as it's said. Our lives were not given freely. Yet we still hope for further boons, maybe win the lottery or be left a large inheritance. It's an interesting exercise to imagine getting everything you want for nothing—a tremendous impediment to spiritual development.

Beelzebub tells his grandson:

> The time of your present age is not given you in which to pay for your existence, but for preparing yourself for the future, for the obligations becoming to a responsible three-brained being. (BT, 77)

We're all at this stage in our development compared to our next step. As such, the best way to prepare to be "a responsible three-brained being" is to learn how the inner and outer universe works. Going off to fix something before fully understanding it ends up making things worse.

According to Beelzebub, there's one thing we can start doing right now: Every morning as you greet the new day try to bring the unconscious parts of yourself in contact with the conscious parts and have a conversation together. Try to convince the unconscious parts not to hinder your spiritual development. Tell them that if you win, everyone wins—but if they win, everyone loses.

CHAPTER EIGHT

THE IMPUDENT BRAT HASSEIN, BEELZEBUB'S GRANDSON, DARES *to* CALL MEN "SLUGS"

This very short chapter, among other things is about right relationship and right effort. Beelzebub is not just going to tell his grandson stories; Hassein must be active to his wish and ask for what he wants. As it's said, you must have skin in the game in order to get anything out of it. Spiritual development requires an extra effort above what life needs from us, and it must come from our own initiative. Inner evolution cannot be coerced. We must ask for what we want. Remember that Jesus Christ promised:

> Ask, and it shall be given to you; seek, and ye shall find; knock, and it shall be opened unto you. For every one that asketh receiveth; and he that seeketh findeth; and to him that knocketh, it shall be opened.[10]

CHAPTER NINE

THE CAUSE *of the* GENESIS *of the* MOON

BEELZEBUB explains that life began on the planet Earth as the "result of the erroneous calculations of certain Sacred Individuals concerned with matters of World-creation and World-maintenance" (BT, 82). A comet starting its first full orbit, and the as-yet unsolidified Earth were on a collision course. The cataclysmic impact sheared off two pieces of the planet. Neither could escape the Earth's influence, and the largest fragment became our Moon, and the smaller became an orbiting aerolite. (This theory about the genesis of the moon is similar to one developed by NASA scientists in the late twentieth century.)

One question raised by this is how can a Sacred Individual make an error, especially one with such catastrophic consequences? Another is, can a human being really be angry at an archangel for making a mistake? This is a useful question to contemplate in terms of forgiving oneself for past mistakes.

Although our solar system finally settled down, some very High Holy Individuals still feared that the new planet and its moons were unstable and could later cause harm to the cosmos. Therefore, a request was submitted to His Endlessness to seed life onto the Earth in the belief that the vibrations of organic life would facilitate the Earth's and moon's solar circulation, ensuring their stability. The request was granted, and life was initiated on Earth. Science theorizes that life started here because small molecules somehow evolved, mixed together, and self-replicated. These "molecules" are the seeds of life that were sown onto the planet.

As for the second moon, which Beelzebub calls Anulios, it was (re)discovered in 2016. Scientists describe it as a quasi-moon called

> Kamo'oalewa, after a Hawaiian word that refers to a moving celestial object.... It circles the Earth in a repeating corkscrew-like trajectory that brings it no closer than 40 to 100 times ... the distance of our more familiar moon. Its odd flight path is caused by the competing gravitational pulls of the Earth and the sun, which continually bend and torque the moonlet's motions, preventing it from achieving a more conventional orbit.[11]

With a little intentional imagination, one can feel the erratic influences coming from Anulios, as Beelzebub says, not allowing anyone to sleep in peace. By Gurdjieff's definition of sleep, this influence might be a contributor to our Divine discontent.

* * *

The Ilnosoparno process is when the Law of Three becomes integrated into a planet, and working on its own, starts producing independent "similitudes-of-the-whole." This is the same moment of conception for every cosmos, from the highest to a single individual human being.

CHAPTER TEN

WHY "MEN" ARE NOT MEN

BEFORE going further, the word *mankind* must be defined. Mankind is a species; from the masculine at one end of the spectrum to the feminine at the other—there are physically, psychically, and spiritually different types of men. So, the word *man* applies to all people. As such a woman is defined as a man with a womb, *a womb-man—woman*. In between these two ends of the scale are all the varieties of difference that compose daily life. That being said, Gurdjieff's speech pattern of always saying "he, him, man, men," or "men-beings" isn't misogynistic. He's referring to all the different kinds of men on the Earth. This is one of the meanings of *equal but different*.

* * *

As the beings on the Earth began to develop, another group of Sacred Individuals returned to the planet to check on its progress. During this visit they perceived something that caused them concern. The Earth beings' instinctive reason was developing more quickly and might outpace their understanding. Certain members of this Most Holy Commission felt that if these three-brained beings too soon discovered the true purpose of their existence—to support the Earth and its new moons—they'd view it as slavery, an untenable position for them, and they'd destroy themselves on principle.

A decision was made to slow down the development of their reason by causing a special organ called Kundabuffer to grow in them. This organ made mankind see everything "topsy-turvy," and made them experience pleasure and enjoyment from all repeated actions.

This can be verified by seeing how little it takes to form a habit. Take a trip somewhere and stop for one reason or another. The next time you take that trip you'll most likely make the same stop.

After several millennia, another Commission returned. They determined that the Earth and moon no longer needed to be supported in the same way, and one of the measures they took was to remove the special organ. However, its consequences had developed "like a Jericho-trumpet-in-crescendo," and today we're still under its effect because of the habits our ancestors developed and passed on. Too late, it was discovered that humanity possessed two traits unique in the whole Megalocosmos. First, the three-brained beings multiplied at an unusually high rate, and second, they periodically destroyed one another's existence.

It's tempting to blame higher forces for our sad situation on Earth: "Why does God let this happen?" However, even after the organ was removed, the consequences stayed through hundreds of generations because of the way we were raised and how we choose to live. Back then, few people took responsibility for their actions or acted from their conscience. Things haven't changed. We want what we want when we want it, and we're not concerned with the future consequences of our desires.

CHAPTER ELEVEN

A PIQUANT TRAIT *of the* PECULIAR PSYCHE *of* CONTEMPORARY MAN

TODAY it's quite evident what happens when someone calls any group by a name they find insulting. Our current cancel culture is nothing but the anathema Beelzebub is explaining with only a few differences. Today's councils are not held solely in churches, town halls, synagogues, etc.—and the presiding authorities aren't the usual establishment "old fossils." Today's courts and councils are spread across the internet on websites, in chat rooms, on opinion shows and every news site. And today, our authorities are anybody with an attractive style, an agenda, and access to an audience. Conviction by these courts means ruination and banishment from public life.

* * *

We are all thin-skinned beings, easily insulted and quick to seek retribution. Why? Interestingly, according to Beelzebub, it's because we're bored and think that we have nothing better to do with our lives.

CHAPTER TWELVE

THE FIRST "GROWL"

As a writer, this chapter raises questions for me about aim and intent. Am I alleviating or adding to His Endlessness' burden? In the story, the writer Beelzebub's referring to isn't important, because he's an archetype that represents the level of understanding we erroneously believe our "authorities" have. This is an important idea to test out in life. Are we spouting some philosophy just because it's in print, widely circulated, and popular? In other words, when we discuss a subject, do we sound more or less like everyone else on one side or the other—repeating the jargon, sound bites, and catch phrases that we like? Or have we developed our own positions based on personal investigation and experience? Individually, can you stand up for your beliefs in the face of enemies and friends?

It's important to begin to see the level of suggestibility that we're under in daily life in order to begin to free ourselves from that influence. That doesn't mean the influence goes away, we just no longer feel its tug as strongly.

CHAPTER THIRTEEN

WHY *in* MAN'S REASON FANTASY MAY BE PERCIEVED *as* REALITY

ONE'S Being-Partkdolg-duty is the conscious labor one does and the intentional suffering undergone in order to deliberate sanely about an issue; thinking for oneself is work. That means willingly accepting responsibility for the consequences of the actions taken based on the facts verified. The truth seeker's mandate is to question everything, because a large part of us wants to let someone else make our decisions. If three people say the same thing to us in the same way, then we know it must be true. Right?

Oddly, today we think that someone who repeats a simple phrase over and over has a clear mind and is a straight talker. This is easy to see when we look at all the catchy expressions that started violent movements or resulted in apathy when action was required. This is suggestibility, a consequence of the organ Kundabuffer, which can only be overcome by Being-Partkdolg-duty.

CHAPTER FOURTEEN

THE BEGINNING *of* PERSPECTIVE PROMISING NOTHING VERY CHEERFUL

IN this chapter Beelzebub relates how, over time, mankind's vibrations grew steadily worse, and great Nature tried to make up for the lack of quality with quantity, another reason for humanity's many population explosions. In my lifetime the world's population has gone from three billion to its current level of almost eight billion. Needless to say, the planet cannot sustain this type of a continuing increase. Like a plague of locusts, people will strip the Earth bare.

* * *

Though people have different types of hair, skin color, etc., that only depends on which part of the planet their ancestors came from. Psychically we all possess the consequences of Kundabuffer to one degree or another. From this comes the belief that everything belongs to us, and we have the right to do with it as we please.

* * *

We will be a warlike people as long as we suffer under suggestibility. For example, Switzerland—where the core principle of its foreign policy is neutrality dictating noninvolvement in any armed or political conflict between other states—supplies the Guard that protects the Pope within Vatican City-State, an independent country. This is an example of mankind's ability to justify anything.

CHAPTER FIFTEEN

THE FIRST DESCENT *of* BEELZEBUB upon the PLANET EARTH

One of this chapter's main themes is taking responsibility, though its's not presented how we typically think about the idea. Although the young naïve countryman's reason is more highly developed than the king's, he has no experience in dealing with the consequences of the organ Kundabuffer. Still, he believes he knows better and makes an agreement signed in blood that binds him and all his tribe to the bargain. (It's an echo of the Transcaucasion Kurd's lack of understanding with more devastating consequences.)

Though Beelzebub seems to do little in the overall process, he is the highest authority there, his Right Reverence, with the most highly developed reason and vast practical experience. He is the organizing principle. Even King Appolis vows to place himself under his authority and accept his judgment. Then they decide on the correct beings to find the best resolution. For Beelzebub's tribe this is a moral obligation because they're of the same blood.

Although it's a difficult principle to grasp, it's true on every planet, including ours. All the indigenous three-brained beings share the same blood, or more precisely, on our planet there are only four types of blood; A, B, AB, and O (the universal donor). And as we saw with the recent pandemic, what effects one affects all. To more or less the same degree we are all internally, psychologically, psychically, and cosmically the same. We seldomly realize that our differences are superficial—like gender, skin color, diet, and other sense-based manifestations.

*   *   *

We want to hold others accountable yet often don't hold ourselves to the same standards. For instance, do I take individual responsibility for wastefulness, or do I let the water constantly run while shaving, brushing my teeth, or washing dishes? It's easy to spot another's lack, but do I do everything possible to curtail my own waste? It's hard not to think that Beelzebub's tribe took things to the extreme; after all, some of them sacrificed their lives to make good on their fellow tribesman's wager. The question is: What do these characters represent in me, and how far am I willing to go to stand behind my beliefs?

* * *

Our simpleton returns to Mars, the symbol of inner struggle, heartbroken and in shame. Later we're told he becomes an excellent bailiff for his tribe. A bailiff is the king's representative, responsible for the administration of the kingdom and the application of justice, both jobs he thought he could already do at the beginning of the tale. This represents a significant growth in his being and understanding from properly and fully digesting those painful events.

CHAPTER SIXTEEN

THE RELATIVE UNDERSTANDING *of* TIME

THIS chapter is an expansion of another idea touched on in the introduction—*time*. Beelzebub calls time an "Ideally-Unique-Subjective-Phenomenon," because:

> Time in itself does not exist, there is only the totality of the results ensuing from all the cosmic phenomena present in a given place. (BT, 123)

In other words, passing time is measured subjectively for a being by the cosmic events surrounding them. On Earth we call one year the time it takes for Earth to make one full rotation around the sun. If we lived on Mercury, one year would be 88 days long—on Mars it would be 687 days, and so on. This measurement of passing time is a fraction of the time of the higher cosmos.

Objective science measures time by a particular event on the Most Holy Sun absolute. Yet this is still subjective for the beings there. However, the time we are most concerned with is the time of our lives, and here we get some distressing news. According to Beelzebub, our ancestors didn't give back to creation on a cosmic level, so they didn't live according to the Foolasnitamnian principal. That level of being is "obliged" to exist until they coat an astral-body in themselves—a soul in the Christian tradition.

Mankind's lifespan needed to be changed to the Itoklanos principal, which is the same for plants and animals whose vibrations only support the local environment (though mankind's don't usually even do that). That's why so many three-brained beings are needed, because their lifelong work of refining energy only produces a droplet of what's needed for world creation and world maintenance.

On the bright side, if we begin to give back on a cosmic level, refining our energies further, we can live fuller (i.e., longer) lives because, as we work toward evolution, time changes. Increasing the fineness of the vibrations we emanate makes us more useful to creation so the available time for us to evolve can lengthen.

CHAPTER SEVENTEEN

THE ARCH-ABSURD ACCORDING *to the* ASSERTION *of* BEELZEBUB, OUR SUN NEITHER LIGHTS NOR HEATS

THIS short, dense chapter begins Beelzebub's teaching about the laws of world creation and world maintenance, forcing us to question our thinking about how the world works. There is far too much knowledge in this chapter to cover in the scope of my aim of providing glimpses into his teaching, so I'll only touch on my favorite ideas.

First is Beelzebub's outrageous pronouncement that our sun not only doesn't heat us directly, but is usually as freezing cold as "the 'hairless-dog' of our highly esteemed Mulla Nassr Eddin." We can begin to grasp this idea if we compare the sun's internal and external temperature with ours. The sun's internal temp is estimated to be 27 million °F, while its surface temp is approximately 10 thousand °F. Putting these values in a ratio to human temperatures, internally we're 98.6°F, which would make our corresponding skin temp -460°F—quite cold indeed. To grow spiritually one must broaden their thinking to include scale and relativity.

* * *

Science still believes the sun is hotter in the summer because it's 3.28 percent closer to the planet, yet how could this slight variation cause the differences between subzero and egg frying temperatures on Earth? Lacking an "instinctive sensing of reality" we're unable to feel that there are other forces involved, although these days one must be willfully ignorant not to see the earth's temp continue to rise while the sun's energy output and distance have remained practically constant.

* * *

Initially, the dwelling place of His Endlessness ran under the Autoegocratic process. Simply put, all force went out from the Most Holy Sun Absolute. His Endlessness discovered that because of this, His dwelling place was shrinking over time—the effect of the Merciless Heropass. To stop the process, His Endlessness changed the two fundamental cosmic laws of the universe so that energies now began to flow back as well as out. This process of reciprocal feeding is called Trogoautoegocratic—I eat Myself. Divinity sends Its creative impulse out and, through its involution and evolution, receives back food for His dwelling place.

We are on the receiving end of this outpouring, and we're designed to take in these vibrations, refine them, and send them back out. One of the gifts from His Endlessness is that we can keep some of that energy for our individual evolution. By intentionally taking in heavier vibrations and digesting them properly, we transform them into the energy needed for our spiritual development.

* * *

In the briefest outline, Heptaparaparshinokh, the Law of Seven, is the law of manifestation—the steps necessary for something to be intentionally brought into being. This idea is exemplified by a musical octave from low do to high do, or the doubling of vibrations that represents a major scale.

Everything that has been or will be created follows this law, and each note represents a step in the process. It's important to know that certain processes are involutionary because the creative impulse starts in a higher world, and then the law unfolds in a downward direction from high do to low do. An evolutionary octave starts from below, striving to rise up to a higher level.

Triamazikamno, the Law of Three, or the law of creation, participates at each note of an octave because three forces are needed to create anything. The creation of the Megalocosmos began with the Divine, dividing into active force, passive force, and neutralizing force. "In the beginning God created the heaven and the earth."[12] God has only Itself to create from, so the first act is one of division. The One becomes Three. It is the mystery of the Christian Trinity.

The Earth passively receives the active creative influence from the Divine, and Heaven acts as neutralizing force, mediating between the other two. These are the same three forces that act on every level of the Megalocosmos, creating an almost infinite number of combinations that continue to expand and maintain existence.

* * *

The initial creative impulse is the Theomertmalogus—the Word of God, or the will of the Absolute, which plunged into the matter of the universe—the prime source substance Etherokrilno, bringing forth Okidanokh, the Omnipresent-Active-Element. This is the Law of Three at the highest creative level.

Rodney Collin (1909–1956), a student of Gurdjieff's work, wrote *The Theory of Celestial Influence*, where he describes the Megalocosmos as having a spherical structure, on one side of which is an *absolute* white-hot pole, and on the opposite side is an *absolute* dark-cold pole. At these poles, radiation and mass

> become entirely separated, the South pole representing . . . pure radiation and the North pole pure mass. Within this sphere are an infinite number of physical conditions, an infinite number of relations to either pole, separated by definite periods [of time].[13]

Filling the space between the two poles is the Omnipresent-Active-Element Okidanokh, which is the three forces blending, separating, and re-blending to create the infinite variety of energy-matter combinations resulting from the south's plunge into the north, filling the world with Life, Form, and Love.

CHAPTER EIGHTEEN

THE ARCH-PREPOSTEROUS

THE first dictionary definition of preposterous is: "contrary to reason or common sense." In this chapter Beelzebub points out a number of preposterous things; for instance, why don't we have a single governing body to make the decisions that affect the welfare of the entire planet's population? This is especially true now that we live in a global community. This, above all else, would soon put an end to war, hunger, climate change, poverty, and all the other social ills currently due to so many divided governments trying to be first. Likewise, why aren't people struggling to reunify with Divinity instead of fighting over who's version of religion is best?

Another preposterous element of this chapter is the work of Gornahoor Harharkh, Beelzebub's essence friend. He's designed and built exceedingly ingenious experimental equipment to delve into the mysteries of the Omni-Present-Active-Element, and he's learned much. Yet, he's literally preforming these experiments separated from everything and destroying parts of Okidanokh in the process. This is akin to how modern scientists work on projects— sequestered from life, believing the ends justify the means. Because of this, not long after, the once cosmically renowned scientist becomes a has-been.

Okidanokh contains the three creative forces in the universe, which are holy, sacred, and necessary to be maintained in a certain ratio for the maintenance and creation of the Megalocosmos. This idea harkens back to Chapter 4 – The Law of Falling, where the three forces are part of "the equilibrium which enables suns and planets to maintain their position" (BT, 66). Gornahoor Harharkh even says that the striving of the three forces to re-blend is what gives planets their stability in the common-system-harmonious-movement (BT, 170). So, intentionally disrupting their possibility of uniformly blending negatively effects everything.

This doesn't bode well for our addiction to electrical energy, which is one of the most harmful aspects of our modern world, both physically and psychologically. Electrical overuse accelerates the negative consequences of climate change, including higher global temperatures and an increase in the frequency of extreme weather events. Yet we continue to extract electricity, only to squander it on lighting up vacant buildings and powering brand-new labor-saving devices. Granted, it's incredibly difficult to live without electricity, as anyone who's experienced a blackout can attest to, but we must appreciate the consequences of this wastefulness.

What's preposterous is that the effects of overconsumption of electricity are all around, and still, we do nothing to reign in these tendencies in ourselves.

*   *   *

Beelzebub is highlighting an unseen repercussion of the wanton extraction of electricity because its production destroys two of the three forces of the creative process, which subsequently unbalances the planet's creative energy. This not only adversely affects the Earth's health, but also humanity's chances of continuing as a species because the air, ground, and water created on the Earth are also out of balance; so certain particles needed for the various processes in us may be very low in number or missing entirely from our foods, particularly those particles needed for coating higher being bodies.

*   *   *

One other preposterous thing in the chapter is Beelzebub's first and last experience of a "criminally egoistic anxiety for the safety of [his] personal existence" (BT, 166). Why? Because it goes against right order. Secrets of the universe are about to be revealed to him, and he's worried if it's going to hurt. We have a deep love for our planetary bodies and wish to keep them in pristine condition up until the moment of our death.

CHAPTER NINETEEN

BEELZEBUB'S TALES ABOUT HIS SECOND DESCENT onto the PLANET EARTH

A commission of Sacred Individuals was concerned that the newly forming atmosphere on the moon was being poisoned by an excess of certain vibrations coming from Earth. One member of the commission asked Beelzebub to sort out this situation on a local level so they didn't have to resort to some extreme sacred process. Beelzebub agreed and set out to stop, or at least curtail, the practice of animal sacrifice on the planet Earth.

I have two personal sore spots in this chapter. The first is when all the beings of Beelzebub's tribe are given a year's warning to leave Atlantis, and so survived the cataclysm. Why wasn't humanity told, so that they could also flee and be saved? The second is when the most-high Archangel Looisos was talking about the three-brained beings who "escaped by accident." Was humanity supposed to end in that cataclysm. Is this where the story of Noah originates? Had humanity fallen so low on the scale of usefulness that things might have been cosmically better off if our ancestors didn't make it?

* * *

> I repeat, all beings, of all brain systems, without exception, large and small, arising and existing on the Earth or within the Earth, in the air or beneath the waters, are all equally necessary for our Common Creator, for the common harmony of the existence of Everything Existing. (BT, 196)

On the scale of a human being, it's hard to imagine one part of the body thinking that another part was unnecessary—and could, and possibly should, be done away with. (I'm not talking about cancers, odd growths, etc.). Then, as part of the Megalocosmos, how can we justify saying one part of creation is less important than another? The eighteenth personal commandment of His Endlessness declares: "Love everything that breathes" (BT, 198).

It's not a sign of love to slaughter other lives to satisfy our inner gods of greed and pleasure. Beelzebub asks a great question: Would the Divine creator of All write, "on the foreheads of certain of His creatures, that they were to be destroyed in His honor and glory?" (BT, 192). Frankly, I wouldn't be surprised to find out that the practice of animal sacrifice was started by religious officials who relied on those kinds of donations for their sustenance.

Although, today, animal sacrifice is generally frowned on, monitored populations of vertebrates (mammals, birds, fish, reptiles, and amphibians) have plummeted on average 69 percent since 1970, according to the World Wildlife Fund's "Living Planet Report of 2022." Much of this is due to deforestation to create the amount of grazing land needed for the cows and sheep we slaughter for food. Ironically, these animals also consume an increasing proportion of worldwide grain production, leaving less of this staple for poorer human populations to eat.

Giant herds of cattle and sheep are significant contributors to water pollution, soil degradation, and greenhouse gas emissions. For instance, the global sheep population is estimated to be about 1.18 billion animals. Each animal can produce an average of 8 gallons of methane a day. Add to that the global cow population, which also numbers over a billion animals, with each producing 40 gallons or more of methane daily. That's almost 50 billion gallons of methane added to the atmosphere every day, day in and day out.

Looking at our modern life through the lens of Gurdjieff's ideas lets us see how topsy-turvy our world is, and our habits of thinking, feeling, and doing that are keeping it that way.

Growing the capacity for conscience in ourselves allows us, like the priest Abdil, to be compassionate and sensitive towards all the other living beings cohabitating on, in, or above the planet. The saying, "We're all God's creatures" is not a catch phrase.

* * *

Much like the many rulers, monarchs, and potentates on this planet, each accidentally separate group also has their own religion or sect, faction, denomination, cult following, etc. The differences in religious teaching are man-made, typically a misunderstanding of higher ideas that have come down by way of a Sacred Messenger from Above, although some religious doctrines are sourced in an unacknowledged mal intent.

Higher truth comes down from the Divine Source and then is disseminated to particular populations, tailored to the times and locations in which they live. If we apply our minds to this study as Gurdjieff asks, we can see that different religions are different ways to know Divinity. The other major differences in our beliefs are consequences of the organ Kundabuffer, which were on full display on a handmade sign some US troops posted at the start of the Iraqi invasion. It read, "My God is better than your God."

Organized religion wants its followers to believe that *only they* have the goods, so to speak. There is no search for higher truth as proved by the catastrophic overt and covert religious wars and persecutions that continue to this day. Also, religion, more than any other influence, is used as a justification for men controlling women in thought and deed.

It is difficult to grasp that many of our religious ideals are a result of the quest for power, riches, and vainglory of men on Earth. Yet, at the heart of every religious teaching is the idea that God is unknowable because of the difference in scale between us and the Divine. Many religions will not even speak the name of Divinity or make an image of that level because it is unpronounceable and unseeable by our level of being. We must be on God's level to even begin to understand Him.

Therefore, anyone professing to know God's will is either on the same level of consciousness as our Endless-Unibeing-Creator, or is under the sway of Kundabuffer. The best indications that we have of Divine will are the messages we receive from conscience. In that place we learn that every part of creation is "equally necessary for our Common Creator, for the common harmony of the existence of Everything Existing" (BT, 196).

CHAPTER TWENTY

THE THIRD FLIGHT *of* BEELZEBUB *to the* PLANET EARTH

Reading this tale requires an open mind and a sense of humor, because it pokes fun at our raw, thinly veiled sensibilities.

> You must know . . . that the beings of the planet Earth are inconceivably proud and touchy. If someone does not share their views or agree to do as they do, or criticizes their manifestations, they are, oh, very indignant and offended. (BT, 233)

As a side note, those words were published seventy-three years ago as of this writing, and this feature has only gotten more entrenched in modern life. There's one thing that almost everyone can agree on today, everybody else is very thin-skinned.

To achieve his aim of eliminating the practice of animal sacrifice, Beelzebub, like King Konuzion before him, uses the feature of suggestibility—following the adage: to be as wise as serpents and as harmless as doves. We want to believe that our religious teachings come directly from God; however, when we do think about Divinity it's from a remarkably low place. It's as if the Almighty Creator of All was only the God of our solar system, or sometimes even only of our little group, and there is nothing living anywhere else.

It takes only a cursory study of any religion's doctrine to find its macho and political aspects. Religious teachings for the most part come from man's interpretation (in most cases, the masculine end of the spectrum) or more precisely their misinterpretation of the words of a Divine messenger. All the major religions of today have come to us after being filtered through various commissions, councils, and committees. All the gospels were written hundreds of years after Christ's death, and codified even later. The first book of the Bible, the Book of Moses, was written long after his passing. Think of the game of telephone, except occasionally someone is intentionally adding to or subtracting from the message. This is how Divine knowledge has been passed down to us.

It's a tough idea to accept that religions are inventions, because they can contain the actual words of a Divine Messenger like Jesus Christ, Moses, Mohamad, Buddha, and others. However, these men and some notable women were not here to start a religion but to teach people how to evolve into consciously useful beings. Our Omnipresent-Unibeing-Endless-Creator does not need blind followers—rather, individual men and woman—to be helpmates.

CHAPTER TWENTY-ONE

THE FIRST VISIT of BEELZEBUB to INDIA

In this new millennium, humanity's tendency to wiseacre has grown to where half of the people will believe anything, and the other half won't believe anything. We've even coined terms like "fake fact" because both sides of any argument use premeditated wiseacring to win their point. It's difficult to grasp the serious effect this feature has until we remember that Christ's teaching, "Love one another" was at times enforced by the Inquisition, the Crusades, the conquistadors, and the torture and murder of millions of women for being witches (or for just being women).

Yet the more indigestible part of this pill is what we believe about ourselves in this life and our possibilities afterward because of the wiseacring of our ancestors. According to Beelzebub, the original teaching of Saint Buddha was to develop a conscious relationship to the Law of Three and the Law of Seven within us so we can begin to coat Divine particles in ourselves—that is, create a soul. In other words, we aren't born with these higher bodies, just the embryo, so to speak, and this grows only through our efforts. This is the meaning behind Gurdjieff's saying:

> Blessed is he that hath a soul; blessed is he that hath none; but grief and sorrow are to him that hath in himself its conception. (BT, 246)

Yet we were brought up to believe that we have a soul, which is constantly fought over by an angel and a devil perched one on each or our shoulders, trying to make us behave well or badly. It's very comforting to think we already have a soul and all we have to do is take it to a building and polish it up once in a while. However, if the idea that we only have a soul in potential is taken rightly, it can be a spur toward inner evolution, because if we don't possess higher being bodies yet, we'd better get started with our Being-Partdolg-Duty.

* * *

One way to intentionally suffer is by bearing the unpleasant manifestations of others. This also requires a conscious effort, as can be clearly seen in the state of the world's political-religious-social landscape. No one wants to make even a simple effort—forget an extra effort—and people would prefer that others suffer, not they themselves. No one cares to listen anymore; we all want to talk and get our point across. Any perceived insult is automatically reacted to internally, and often externally, which accounts for the overall unrest, and the numerous random acts of extreme violence in the world today.

However, it's taught that our thin skin can become an asset if we use it properly, and not let it use us. One way is to intentionally bear the unpleasant manifestations of others, which is a process of digestion similar to the Archangel Hariton's system, transforming the heavy matter of our life into the finer energy matters for coating and perfecting higher-being bodies.

CHAPTER TWENTY-TWO

BEELZEBUB *for the* FIRST TIME *in* TIBET

I initially thought that certain sections of this chapter were metaphorical, like when he talks about the Himalayan Mountains being so high that they cause the planet's earthquakes. I believed there had to be some hidden meaning in this tale, like maybe the monks were so high above their neighbors that they were out of touch with the world, and this was causing more harm than good. I figured something like this because, obviously, other planets never passed within the earth's atmosphere: The closest planet is tens of millions of miles away. Then I came across this recent quote in the Journal of Coastal Conservation:

> Planets interact with each other influencing earthquakes via the gravitational stresses arising from the configuration of the solar system planets that cause a slowdown of the rotational/revolving speed of the Earth. This stimulates the Earth's plate to move generating earthquake[s] due to the activation of faults.[14]

It's said there are seven levels of meaning in Beelzebub's tales. It's important to consider that one of them might be the factual, but that's up to us to verify for ourselves.

* * *

We live in a world ruled by sects of various religions that condone silencing anyone who doesn't follow their teachings. They willingly sacrifice husbands, wives, children, parents, and friends to a misinterpretation of real truth. Besides the outright holy wars on our planet like the Crusades, the conquest of the Americas, the Rwandan genocide, and many others, there have been numerous suicide bombings, mass shootings, abductions of whole classes from schools that teach girls—as well as the ongoing attacks on women, including forced marriage, slave labor, honor killings, dress police, child brides, genital mutilation, and extreme punishments like facial disfigurement and stoning, which are all religiously inspired.

How far is this from Jesus Christ's teaching:

> And thou shalt love the Lord thy God with all thy heart, and with all thy soul, and with all thy mind, and with all thy strength ... [and] Thou shalt Love thy neighbour as thyself. (Mark, 12:30–31, KJV)

Or from Muhammad's teaching that

> God is so loving that He recreated His attribute of love as an instinct in us. Hence true love is part of God's love, and it is our duty to love one another truly, as indeed He loves us.[15]

*   *   *

Another side of this coin is following the monastic lifestyle, and "suffering-in-solitude." It's easier to hide in a hole and slowly die of deprivation than to struggle with daily life, striving to be useful to creation in the midst of one's day-to-day experiences. This is the driving force behind the construction of virtual worlds, which are so titillating to modern sensibilities. We get the thrills and chills of life with no effort on our part. It's the same as everyone wanting a quick and effort-free way into heaven. Sorry, there is none. We're told that

Divinity is in a constant struggle between desires and non-desires. Should we be any different?

Struggling against our base desires in the midst of our life is being useful to the Creator by easing His burden. Doing what we feel like regardless of the consequences (both internal and external) is adding to His Endlessness' burden.

CHAPTER TWENTY-THREE

THE FOURTH PERSONAL SOJOURN of BEELZEBUB on the PLANET EARTH

How are we to understand Mullah Nassr Eddin's quote, "The cause of every misunderstanding must be sought only in women"? Was Gurdjieff a misogynist? If so, why did he entrust a woman, Jeanne de Salzmann with the continuation of his work? When the words *man* and *woman* are used, there arise in us deeply habitual sentiments from thousands of years of religion-inspired patriarchal doctrine. Is Gurdjieff simply retelling the story of Eve, who was blamed for the fall of mankind?

In discussing Exioëhary, Beelzebub says that the inhabitants of the Earth, "call it sperm" (BT, 275). In this context it sounds like a kind of male superiority—men have it and women don't. Only later does he explain that members of both the male and female sex produce this sacred cosmic substance. Once again, a woman's body is a mystery, which is why this substance is practically unknown in them. For Beelzebub, the sex of a being is only one of their determining factors, one which makes the person more receptive to certain forces than they are to others.

Another difference between men and women is that each sex has different obligations to creation. For instance, women are given the responsibility for the race of mankind because it is brought forth and mainly cared for by them. As it's said not always jokingly—if men had babies, there would've been only one generation.

So, is there truth in Mullah Nassr Eddin's saying, "the cause of every misunderstanding must be sought only in woman"? From one perspective this means that all our "problems" come from Holy

Denying Force. Beelzebub explains to his grandson how two of the three holy forces of creation are embodied in two different sexes: active force in men, receptive force in women. These forces act on their own through the beings who are embodying them at the time, and these forces have consequences. Until we become aware of the forces that drive us, we will be semiconscious puppets at the mercy of life's whims.

*   *   *

Being only marginally aware of the 1925 Scopes trial, which was popularly called "the Monkey Trial," I did some research. The great civil liberties lawyer Clarence Darrow (1857–1938) won his case, allowing evolution to eventually be taught in schools. I thought that was that. Then I found the following quote on the Smithsonian Museum of Natural History's Frequently Asked Questions website updated July 11, 2022, and realized that the question of who came from whom is still an issue today.

> Humans and monkeys are both primates. But humans are *not* descended from monkeys or any other primate living today. We *do* share a common ape ancestor with chimpanzees. It lived between 8 and 6 million years ago. But humans and chimpanzees evolved differently from that same ancestor. All apes and monkeys share a more distant relative, which lived about 25 million years ago.

Was this "common ape ancestor" around in the time on Earth being examined by Beelzebub? After all, there can't be only one ancestor of a new species, two different beings come together to beget a third type of being—a hybrid. If that's the case, how different is science's theory to what Beelzebub is saying? Could this common ancestor have been created at a time when, because of certain planetary and cosmic conditions, humans and animals could interbreed?

Also, it's not like people don't still do it. In the United States bestiality only became a federal crime in the 1950s. Also, science asserts that on the human evolutionary scale, our earliest ancestors weren't that far from being animals themselves.

Beelzebub's Tales is meant to disrupt our usual ways of thinking and force us to reexamine all that we've been told and accepted without personal verification. We are given Belcultassi as an example of someone verifying everything. While contemplating on the sense and aim of his existence, Belcultassi discovered something not quite right in him. Through incredible "organic and psychic efforts" he achieved the potency to be sincere with himself, and then began to take stock, so to speak. During his impartial analyzation Belcultassi discovered that his manifestations were unbecoming. This is again the passage from Romans 7:19, KJV: "For the good that I would, I do not: but the evil which I would not, that I do."

To check his work, and find a way out of this condition, he gathered like-minded beings and compared notes. This led to the creation of a school for all those who felt and thought this same way, and together they sought a way out of their situation.

We like to believe that we are at least sincere with ourselves, but a critical evaluation of our thoughts, feelings, and deeds may show us otherwise. While most people feel there is something wrong with the world, and some set out to try and fix it, few think to look at their inner world. Do we ever wonder if there's something wrong in there that we might be able to fix, which would change our outer life as well?

The result of Belcultassi's efforts was that he became a saint, a being on a very high level of usefulness to creation. As a side benefit of his work, the Society of the Akhaldans was formed, and because of their efforts "genuine objective science just then arose and began to exist for the first time" on the Earth (BT, 298). According to Beelzebub, after Atlantis sank, a few surviving members of this learned society migrated to Egypt. There they strove to revive their society and created the great sphinx at the entrance to their school. This of course makes the monument thousands of years older than modern Egyptologists will accept. However,

> in 1992, John Anthony West rocked the scientific community with his claim that the Sphinx was actually carved 10,000 years earlier, before Egypt was a desert. West and others argued that academia had overlooked an important detail—the body of the sculpture bore distinct markings of water erosion.[16]

This estimate is more in line with Beelzebub's timeline, as well as explaining his description of the fertile valley where these former Akhaldans settled. One reason for a lack of academic interest in discovering a possible earlier date for the creation of the sphinx is that we'd know without equivocation that there was a civilization on Earth more technologically, psychologically, and spiritually advanced than ours. This is an awful blow to our self-importance that shakes the foundations of our belief that we are at the pinnacle of all the civilizations that preceded us.

CHAPTER TWENTY-FOUR

BEELZEBUB'S FLIGHT *to the* PLANET EARTH *for the* FIFTH TIME

For this chapter I simply wish to highlight some definitions:
- War: The process of reciprocal destruction that, considering all the beings populating the entire created universe, only occurs on the planet Earth. I believe that our indulgence in this process was likely one reason Beelzebub's tribesmen didn't warn our ancestors about the coming cataclysm. They were directed from above not to reveal cosmic truths to our ancestors because they couldn't comprehend them rightly with their low being. Remember what Albert Einstein unwittingly created with a little inspiration.
- Learned Being: A being who acquires "by their conscious labors and intentional sufferings the ability to contemplate the details of creation from the point of view of World-arising, and World-existence" (BT, 322). These are the big questions—who am I, and what is my purpose here?—that we usually stop asking shortly after puberty.
- Learned Being of New Format: A being who "'learned-by-rote' as much as possible about every kind of vacuous information, [including] that half a hundred is fifty" (BT, 323). Sadly, this describes most of us and the accumulated knowledge we treasure.
- Human Happiness: Acquiring "for their own possession a great deal of that popular metal there called 'gold'" (BT, 324). What else is there to say except check your personal definition.

- Hasnamuss: A being who *has-no-must*. Everything they do is for self-gratification and their own glorification. People with the consequences of the organ Kundabuffer fully crystalized in them, with no hint of conscience remaining in them.
- The Sorcerer's Secret: A maleficent fiction, corrupting the real idea of transmutation, which is turning our inner course material into finer energy matters.
- Egyptian Priest: A descendant of a member of the Society of Akhaldan who has continued to strive to fulfill their ideals. This is the reason the image of an Egyptian Priest has such a mystique for us. They've entered into our folklore as magicians and sorcerers because we don't understand how they possibly did the things they did, like build the pyramids.
- Soul, Heaven, and Hell, according to Beings of the Earth:
  Soul—a higher body within that was born with them, and after death will be held accountable for their actions in life and rewarded or punished accordingly.
  Heaven—The place a "good" soul goes, where the carnal desires they sacrificed during life will now be fulfilled many times over with free food and drink and sex any time they like with virgins at their beck and call.
  Hell—The horrible place a "bad" soul goes if the person indulged their carnal desires in their lifetime. This is for all eternity, and the soul will suffer as if it was a corporeal body being endlessly tortured.
- Tower-of-Babel: Adding another B in the middle of the last word gives the gist of its meaning. Discussions about "questions of the beyond" are beyond our reason until, like Hamolinadir, we seek to understand through conscious effort and intentional suffering how and why the world

works as it does and the possible higher levels of existence awaiting us.
- Objective Good and Bad:
    Good—Every action done according to conscience.
    Bad—An action from which a person experiences remorse of conscience.
- Subjective Good: A modern moral concept that depends "on the moods of the local authorities, which moods in their turn depend also automatically on the state of the four sources of action existing there under the names 'mother-in-law,' 'digestion,' 'John Thomas,' and 'cash'" (BT, 343)—today called fear, food, sex, and money.

CHAPTER TWENTY-FIVE

THE VERY SAINTLY ASHIATA SHIEMASH, SENT *from* ABOVE *to the* EARTH

Frist, I'd like to share some work done by my dear departed essence friend, Andy. He was very religious, and when he noticed something familiar in the name Ashiata Shiemash, he searched for connections between Gurdjieff's tales and Hebrew teachings. The following are some notes from his study that show both the depths of Gurdjieff's world, and one man's effort to plumb them:

> *Ashiata*: the A is a breath sound, like Aleph in Hebrew. It is an exhalation, or the push of the creative and regenerative impulse into the world. SH is the sound in the word Shin, which means water, representing the receptive half of the universe. IA is pronounced like Yah, one of the holy names of G-d. ATA equals Atah, which can be read as I-Art/Thou-You. *Shiemash*: SH is water representing higher knowledge, Yah is another of G-d's sacred names. M, or Mem equals Water as Truth. EMA is mother, and ASH could be the result of burning, but it also stands for the first man and woman.

Andy went on for another four pages on the different Hebrew words and concepts contained within the name Ashiata Shiemash, including the three mothers who gave birth to the tree of life, the candle lighter who shows the way for others, the bearer of the water of life, and the fire of creation. He concluded that because the name was so rich in meaning, it could only be considered an angelic utterance.

* * *

"By the All Most Gracious Command of Our omni-loving common father endlessness... [Ashiata Shiemash] became a difinititized conception of a sacred Individual" (BT, 347). This is possibly a description of implanting the seed of a sacred Individual in a fertile human embryo so that it could grow up and struggle with the consequences of Kundabuffer in itself, in order to understand how best to help people overcome it in themselves. Ashiata Shiemash was the most "successful" of all the messengers in passing on this knowledge because he didn't preach to the masses, so a religion never rose up around him. Instead, he insured that his teachings passed on unpolluted by giving them only to initiates who were properly prepared by him or his direct initiates.

Gurdjieff is passing this knowledge on to us, which is another reason for his difficult-to-understand writing style. We have to work to get it so that we get it the right way.

CHAPTER TWENTY-SIX

THE LEGOMINISM CONCERNING *the* DELIBERATIONS *of the* VERY SAINTLY ASHIATA SHIEMASH UNDER *the* TITLE *of* "THE TERROR-*of-the*-SITUATION"

THE terror of the situation is that our Sacred Being impulses of faith, love, and hope, which should be able to initiate our self-development, have been thoroughly corrupted be the way we live. We have faith in our thoughts and feelings, though they are untested. This might seem unbelievable until you think about how many times we've been disastrously wrong because of believing we were right.

Our love of feeling, he says, actually evokes the opposite. In part, this is the level of relationship we have with everything—love-hate. Even our most beloved darling sometimes drives us crazy. But worse than the degradation of these Divine impulses is the sad condition of the sacred impulse of hope, which has turned into the disease of tomorrow, forestalling us taking action until it's too late. When we finally decide to do something, we sadly no longer have the energy for it.

At the same time, we all know, though won't admit, that we're going to grow old and die—as my father used to say, if we're lucky. Yet we believe, under the influence of today's marketing, that we can maintain youth, vim, vigor, and vitality as long as we use certain products. Based on the deliberations of the Saintly Ashiata Shiemash, this faith in the body is stupidity.

Through intense labors and sufferings, the Saintly Ashiata Shiemash comes to understand that the people he's been sent here to help can rid them themselves of Kundabuffer's consequences if conscience participates in their daily consciousness. This is a very commonsensical conclusion. If we all acted from conscience, could the world be in the condition it's in today?

CHAPTER TWENTY-SEVEN

THE ORGANIZATION *for* MAN'S EXISTENCE CREATED *by the* VERY SAINTLY ASHIATA SHIEMASH

BEELZEBUB explains that conscience is the accumulation of the particles of the "emanations-of-the-sorrow" of our "Omni-Loving and Long-Suffering-Endless-Creator," resulting from His struggle between desires and non-desires. That's why conscience is called the "Representative of the Creator." When we participate in that same struggle, we are assisting the Creator's work, and when we're not, we're adding to His burden and sorrow.

Under the Saintly Ashiata Shiemash's organizing principles, people started living directed by conscience, and as a result they created a utopia. Positions of power and authority were held by beings who merited them by the quality of their manifestations. The heinous practice of dividing each other into casts and classes fell away on its own. People lived longer because they put out finer vibrations, becoming more useful to Nature and higher cosmoses. This meant that fewer vibrations were required, so the birthrate also dropped. People reproduced according to cosmic principles, not just from lust or odd religious practices.

During the days when people lived by the teachings of the Saintly Ashiata Shiemash, they treated each other as fellow vessels for the accumulation of the particles of His Endlessness' sorrow. Each person, according to their level of being and understanding strove to substantiate in themselves the five "being-obligolnian-strivings."

- The first striving: to have in [our] ordinary being existence

everything satisfying and really necessary for [our] planetary body.
- The second striving: to have a constant and unflagging instinctive need for self-perfection in the sense of being.
- The third: the conscious striving to know ever more and more concerning the laws of World-creation and World-maintenance.
- The fourth: the striving from the beginning of [our] existence to pay for [our] arising and [our] individuality as quickly as possible, in order afterward to be free to lighten as much as possible the Sorrow of our Common Father.
- And the fifth: the striving always to assist the most rapid perfecting of other beings, both those similar to oneself and those of other forms, up to the degree of the sacred "Martfotai," that is, up to the degree of self-individuality. (BT, 386)

An interesting and useful experiment is to write out the strivings on a small piece of paper and keep it with you, in case you want to look them over during your day.

CHAPTER TWENTY-EIGHT

THE CHIEF CULPRIT *in the* DESTRUCTION *of* ALL *the* VERY SAINTLY LABORS *of* ASHIATA SHIEMASH

LENTROHAMSANIN represents an archetype. He is the author of the philosophy of self-interest and self-service. If Ayn Rand had been popular at the time *Beelzebub's Tales* was written, her name might also have gone into its makeup. There may be a few other candidates for inclusion in this name, but I offer these four: Lenin, Trotsky, Ham, and Sanin.

Lenin and Trotsky are the authors of the Russian Revolution, which in their minds (or their words, at least) was a striving for pure communism: a stateless, classless, egalitarian union of workers free from exploitation, controlling their own destiny. In reality, more than 50 million people were put to death striving to bring that dream about, which never became reality. This was clearly seen in the years following when the egalitarian union had to build walls to stop their citizens from escaping.

Ham could be a biblical reference. He was Noah's son who disrespected his father by reveling in his apparent drunken foolery. There are numerous interpretations of Ham "seeing his father's nakedness," everything from him performing sodomy on his father to castrating him. Yet at the root of every interpretation is his dishonoring his father: breaking the Fifth Commandment. Ham has no sense of shame and puts his own wants and desires above all others, even those of the Divine, his father, and his family.

Sanin might possibly refer to a character in a book with the same title written by the Russian author and playwright Mikhail

Artsybashev (1878–1927). The book espouses sex for its own sake—do it because it feels good. It's similar to the free love movement of the 1960s in America, which ended with the AIDs epidemic. One character sums up his philosophy in the line, "life was the realization of freedom, and consequently it was natural for a man to live for enjoyment." This book is still available today, and apparently had an enormous impact on the country's youth. It's publication almost instantly brought about a "sexual revolution" that allowed Russian youths to ignore their sense of organic shame.

In regards to Lentrohamsanin's Kashireitleer, or manifesto: First, he is very rich and basically buys his standing among the learned beings of new format. He overwhelms their senses with food and drink and then shows them something none of them have ever seen because no one ever thought to create one before. This type of "stupefaction" happens to us with the release of each new product or service that comes to market. We're dazzled by the sights and sounds of advertising, and if one of our friends starts to talk up the new thing and how wonderful it is, we're soon on board. This is the phenomena of a successful ad campaign sweeping all common sense aside and starting a craze.

One way to tell that the Learned Beings of New Format are taken in or hypnotized by the presentation is because not one of them spots any contradictions in his manifesto or its lack of a firm stand on any issue except the overthrow of the present government so that they can all be free. All of his statements are in "politician-speak," promising much but providing little detail.

The freedom Lentrohamsanin espoused is tempting because it offers something for nothing. He was astute in reading people's base desires and quickly gathered a hard-core following. This same psychological trait has bloomed in different beings over and over on the planet, most recently in America. A leader promises to uphold people's individual rights and remove all restrictions from their freedom, which are usually someone else's fault. The problem is how freedom is interpreted: Usually it's the right to do whatever I want, regardless of the rights of the rest of the citizens around me wishing to live in peaceful cooperation, and get a little ahead.

Lentrohamsanin is an eternal Hasnamuss because he cannot rid himself of the impulses he's internalized, including:

- Every kind of depravity, conscious as well as unconscious;
- The feeling of self-satisfaction from leading others astray;
- The irresistible inclination to destroy the existence of other breathing creatures;
- The urge to become free from the necessity of actualizing the being-efforts demanded by Nature;
- The attempt by every kind of artificiality to conceal from others what in their opinion are one's physical defects;
- The calm self-contentment in the use of what is not personally deserved;
- The striving to be not what one is.

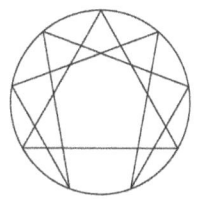

BOOK TWO

CHAPTER TWENTY-NINE

THE FRUITS *of* FORMER CIVILIZATIONS *and the* BLOSSOMS *of the* CONTEMPORARY

Is Gurdjieff oversimplifying in this chapter or cutting to the essence of the situation? Since their fall we've heard about the greatness of the Greco-Roman civilization and the benefits we've inherited from them. Yet, what do we actually know about these ancient folk? When we think of their so-called triumphs, as with all former relationships we remember the good parts. The bad parts usually get swept under the, "that's ancient history" rug.

The philosophical Golden Age of ancient Greece came about because of one man, Socrates (470–399 BCE). Ironically, later in life he was tried, convicted, and sentenced to death by his fellow Greeks for a trumped-up charge of impiety: failing to acknowledge the city's gods, and introducing new deities. These were similar charges to those brought against Jesus Christ at His trial.

A well-known saying of Socrates is, "Wisdom is knowing you know nothing." Regarding the other famous philosophers of the time, as Beelzebub said, they're "pouring from the empty into the void" (BT, 413). "What! Heresy," you cry. "What about Aristotle and Plato?" Well, Plato is most famous for writing down the words of Socrates, even though he didn't heed them himself. He invented the dialectic method, which is a discussion between two or more people, trying to figure out which one of them is right. This is not proceeding as if you know nothing.

Aristotle was Plato's student, and he followed his teacher's example, drawing on his own knowledge to solve problems. He is called "the father of logic," which is the justification of a premise using reason—essentially thinking you know and talking until you prove it to yourself and others. To pass any debate course one must be able to logically argue both sides of a proposition to a win. In terms of seeking real wisdom, this is a perfect example of pouring from the empty into the void, which is repeatedly proven in any number of courtrooms where the innocence or guilt of a person is less important than how well their lawyer reasons. It is interesting to note that the arch-vainglorious Alexander was tutored by Aristotle.

Both of these philosophies blended with modern science have directly or indirectly led to "blessings" like the arguments for limitless use of pesticides, plastics, and petroleum products—along with those advocating the building and deployment of chemical, biological, and nuclear weapons. Albert Einstein only understood the consequences of his efforts after seeing the devastation nuclear weapons wreaked on the nonmilitary, densely populated, Japanese cities of Hiroshima and Nagasaki. He said, "If I had known, I would have become a watchmaker."

* * *

The Roman civilization was decadent to its core, filled with corruption and violence. It was built on the backs of slaves, which some estimates put at 25 percent of Rome's population at its peak. This lack of shame extended to Rome's military, which was especially brutal, having killed by hand with sword and spear some 15 million people at a time when the entire world's population averaged 200 million.[15] That's over 7 percent, not including another half-million or so people who met brutal deaths for public entertainment in their famous sports arena, the Coliseum.

* * *

Roman debauchery is legendary. We've all heard the names of emperors who made sexual extravagance an art form. The most flagrant examples would be Caligula, Tiberius, and Nero—and in the case of Claudius, his wife, Valeria Messalina. Yet, though their brand of hedonism was the most extravagant, sexual perversion seeped into all aspects of Roman life. And these ideas were spread throughout their empire alongside the rest of their culture. The word pornography dates back to these times, a "gift that keeps on giving" today.

> Forty million Americans regularly visit porn sites, and 35% of internet downloads are pornography related. Among all adolescents, pornography hinders the development of a healthy sexuality, and among adults distorts sexual attitudes and social realities.[17]

Sadly, these numbers are clearly increasing.

* * *

Besides our lack of organic shame and the confusion of our reasons, another blossom of these former "great" civilizations is the modern strategy of reciprocal destruction. Eric Arthur Blair (1903–1950) was better known by his pen-name George Orwell. Blair had the faculty to see the trends of his time and predict their logical trajectories into the future. He was particularly accurate with the ways future war would be fought—small-scale terrorist attacks on civilian populations followed by a government's large-scale, armed-military response. Though the threat of an unstable person launching nuclear weapons still exists, the new face of warcraft is an almost continuous process on a smaller scale.

* * *

Beelzebub has given us an opportunity to see the extent to which we're under this insidious influence of suggestibility, and how to shield ourselves from its maleficent effects. But because of how our existence has had to be modified by great Nature for cosmic purposes, he also tells us we have limited time. If we study and practice the idea of a regulator, we can intentionally "unwind" our brains more slowly, making the most of our time. One way to do this is to exercise each of our brains daily. In other words, do something intellectual, emotional, and physical each day. In other words, when "tackling" a problem, work on it with more than one brain. This is one way to fulfill our own higher purpose while fulfilling Nature's need.

Something to remember: *negativity unwinds a center faster.*

CHAPTER THIRTY

ART

The dictionary defines art as the expression or application of human creative skill and imagination that produces works to be appreciated primarily for their beauty or emotional power. Compare this with the opening remarks at the founding of the Adherents-of-Legominism when the term Art was first coined:

> If we contemporary men desire at the present time to do something beneficent for men of future times, all we must do is just to add to [the] already existing means of transmission some new means. (BT, 459)

The point is that because the ancient lines of transmitting knowledge were failing, they were trying to find an *artificial* way of passing on real knowledge to future generations. This is the aim of objective science: intentionally creating something to benefit our children's children's children. This chapter is a deep hard look at how far away from that aim our modern world has gotten with its almost complete focus on instant personal gratification. Ironically, Gurdjieff is writing about his world of a hundred years ago. Have we progressed?

* * *

It's easy to grasp Beelzebub's talk about mankind losing the ability to see reality. Roy G. Biv is an age-old anagram that was used to remember the colors of the visible light spectrum: red, orange, yellow, green, blue, indigo, and violet. Recently there's been a movement in the scientific community to eliminate indigo from the rainbow because the human eye does not now readily see hues in the wavelengths between blue and violet:

> Modern physics generally accepts a six-color spectrum. Indigo is omitted because few people can differentiate the wavelengths well enough to see it as a separate color.[18]

This is a documented diminishment of mankind's ability to see reality—something our recent ancestors could do that we can't. The Adherents-of-Legominism understood the Law of Seven, and used it to conceal real knowledge of past events on the Earth for future generations to discover. The law was well-known at the time in all aspects of daily life, so they believed that the embedded real knowledge would pass from generation to generation. However, in our time we're even wiseacring with representations of the Law of Seven, the fundamental cosmic law of creation. This diminishes further any chance of finding the knowledge hidden within.

The only apparent aim in the minds of the scientists of New Format is toiling away at producing profitable products and fame-inducing discoveries and inventions. This is obvious when we stop to consider the number of wrongful death suits, false advertising claims, and general dissatisfaction with products that never live up to their hype. How many items are rushed to market before their long-term consequences are even known? This is working for the present, for immediate reward and satisfaction.

* * *

Very briefly, the Law of Seven contains the steps necessary to manifest something. For example, a musical octave goes from low do to high do, continuously increasing its vibrations (although not uniformly) until they double, creating a complete scale. Everything follows this law, and each note represents a step in the process. Sadly, beyond thinking about our work week and occasionally lucky lottery numbers—we're unaware of this universal law today.

Why don't we seek the knowledge of our remote ancestors as we marvel at the shards of the remarkably high civilizations they left behind? The Adherents-of-Legominism understood that the Law of Seven would exist as long as the universe existed. It was so prevalent in their everyday life that they didn't realize that over time even this knowledge would "utterly fail" to reach contemporary three-brained beings. We've lost a key to unlock ancient knowledge, so when we see these wonders, we have no idea what they're trying to tell us.

* * *

Beelzebub's Tales to His Grandson is a Legominism. That's one of the things our daily consciousness finds so jarring when we read his stories. But, if we take his ideas into our life and refuse to accept or deny anything until we're fully satisfied by our reason, it opens us up to receive higher influences. For instance, have I tried to observe three separate brains in myself? Have I ever experienced thinking about something in a positive way and feeling bad about the same thing? This is not one brain with two thoughts, but two different brains weighing in on the subject. And if we look closely, we'll find that during this debate, the moving/instinctive brain is considering possibilities with the opposite sex, the quality and/or quantity of food available, and its current level of comfort.

It's not a stretch to say that we are physically one type of being, emotionally another type, and a third type intellectually. This is the reason we have "three totally different kinds of being impulses ... in and on the same whole presence" (BT, 481). In other words, we've developed three different personalities based on these three brains, each with a different take on life. This wreaks havoc on our ability to make our aims or even get along well in the world. It's said that when a couple weds, at least six people are getting married together.

* * *

Beelzebub's scathing inditement of modern theaters and the "poor" actors who populate them must include today's big- and little-screen movies, social media productions, radio shows, and other such output—and the various shining stars and polished celebrities who perform for us on them.

A key factor in determining the level of a person's being is what they are working for. If someone is working for the benefit of future generations, that indicates higher levels of consciousness and being. Interestingly, Ahoon steps into the narrative at this point to give Hassein advice. One thing Beelzebub's old faithful servant represents is personality, which in Beelzebub's case has acquired the practical knowledge of how to deal with the features of self-importance, vanity, and the rest of Kundabuffer's consequences when working toward an aim.

We interact with life through our personalities, and if they're rich, full, and rightly educated they can help our higher self through life's dangers onto higher aims. This goes back to the idea of being sheep in a world of wolves and learning how to be as wise as serpents while striving to be as harmless as doves.

CHAPTER THIRTY-ONE

THE SIXTH *and* LAST SOJOURN *of* BEELZEBUB *on the* PLANET EARTH

Is there a more mature perspective of man's predisposition to war? The first-time guns were used in a war was in 1331, and their use became widespread by the 1400s. Now, almost 700 years later, we continue to sacrifice our children to advancements in the process of reciprocal destruction. We look at war heroes as courageous beings to be emulated; yet according to Beelzebub's observations, cowardice and self-preservation are key elements of their makeup.

This can be verified with a little self-examination. Take for instance the situation where you're driving along and someone cuts you off or rides your bumper. You have to be quick to see it, but the first response is typically fear—they're endangering you (either perceived or imagined). Almost immediately that turns to anger as the impulse for self-preservation kicks in, leading to a habitual response of violence, either externally or internally. This is justified by a twist in the old Bible saying, "Doing to them what they did to you." Our adrenaline is pumping, and it happens so fast that our foot is on the gas or brake pedal before any thinking can occur.

Who is the more heroic soldier? The one who charges into enemy fire trying to save himself, or a conscientious objector who serves honorably in a front-line mobile field hospital. Our higher selves know that killing another living being is an act against the Creator. Yet strangely, we've accepted the premise that war is an inevitable condition of mankind. Why?

* * *

We typically judge our worth as a human being based on what we believe others think and feel about us. Subsequently, we're in an almost constant state of comparison based on imagination. This contributes to us being thin-skinned people, which is a problem for those who wish to evolve, because a sense of humor, especially about oneself, is needed to spiritually awaken.

*   *   *

Another consequence of Kundabuffer is that when we feel remorse for a thought or feeling we've had or an action we took, there arises in us the "god of self-calming." We innately do not like agitation in our lives, and like water, we seek the easiest path. Under the guidance of this inner "god of self-calming," we can make up all kinds of excuses and justify any previous behavior. This allows us to continue on our way, knowing whatever it was, it wasn't our fault.

*   *   *

If Leonardo Da Vinci had been a doctor, he'd likely have been on his way to becoming a Zirlikner, the beings who

> [take] upon themselves essential obligations in relation to the environment of beings similar to themselves ... [and devote] the whole of their existence to helping any being of that region to fulfill his being-obligations. (BT, 541)

A Zirlikner sees their fellow beings from a high perspective, looking at the entirety of the being, their required functions, and purpose as well as the immediate and higher environments they occupy. Sadly, because of what we've accepted as higher learning, our medical profession is separated into different disciplines, each having professionals with varying levels of competence. In America there are 135 medical specialties, 13 mental health professions, and

51 PhD degrees, all entitling the bearer to be called "doctor," and one only has to be two-thirds right to graduate.

In contrast, Zirlikners devote themselves to helping fellow beings become harmonized parts of the whole. In terms of healing, they care for a being's planetary body, their environment, and their possibilities of individual evolution.

* * *

The ability to be sincere with ourselves comes from feeling remorse and letting it burn but not ruin us, so it can be used as a permanent reminding factor. Without an honest measurement of our self-worth, which takes impartial measurement and evaluation, we are unable to place ourselves correctly on the path to individual evolution, making us unable to see our next step.

CHAPTER THIRTY-TWO

HYPNOTISM

The dictionary defines hypnotism as the induction of an alternate state of consciousness where a person apparently loses the power of voluntary action, becoming responsive to suggestion or direction. It's typically used in mental health therapy to recover suppressed memories or allow the modification of behavior by suggestion.

According to Beelzebub, humans are the only beings in the universe who can be hypnotized, because of how we're raised. The education given to us by parents, relatives, teachers, TV, radio, the internet, and friends fills us with confrontative data that we're taught never to confront—only accept. "Why? Because I said so." Luckily, there's another consciousness buried in us called the subconscious, in which our finer impulses have taken refuge.

Because these two consciousnesses are disconnected from each other, it creates the unique situation that if one of them is awake, the other is asleep. One result of this is that if in our daily life we recognize something "off" (i.e., receive a message from conscience nestled in our subconscious), our daily consciousness either quickly forgets the perception or chalks it up to circumstances beyond its control or someone else's problem/fault/responsibility. In other words, if we catch a glimpse of something distasteful in our being, we look for someone or something else to blame, yet conscience is our connection to the Divine, where we find the truth of our being.

When someone is put under hypnosis, they are in fact having their daily consciousness "put to sleep," allowing their subconscious to awaken. According to Beelzebub, this hypnotic state is brought on by a change in blood flow, which is not a directional change in the cells' movement but an activation of the "blood of the Kesdjan body," or the soul.

Beelzebub differentiates between a fully formed Kesdjan body and one in potential, which most of us have. To permanently coat a fully formed Kesdjan body, or grow a soul in us, is one aim of the spiritual journey. This higher body in us is embryonic, having all the basic functions for life, including a circulatory system. When that's stimulated, or as Beelzebub says, its blood starts to flow, the body Kesdjan becomes active, and our subconscious begins to surface out of its magical enchantment.

From one perspective, the subconscious is at an early stage of development, which may be part of the reason for its openness to suggestion. Hypnotism is proven to be successful in altering certain behaviors, but because the change is induced from without, there's often no conscious memory of what took place. The experience may cure a detrimental habit, but it's not useful for inner development. The soul grows from conscious labor and intentional suffering. When its blood flows, we are connected to our real self, our real life, and our real possibilities. It's better to do that wide-awake.

Interestingly, the disorders that hypnotism helps cure—like addiction to opium, hashish, and alcohol, among others—are ways people separate themselves further from reality, separating their two consciousnesses farther apart.

CHAPTER THIRTY-THREE

BEELZEBUB *as* PROFESSIONAL HYPNOTIST

In order to evolve we must begin to see the hypnotism of our modern life. America in particular has become a melting pot for the world's vices. The US has the highest rate of illegal drug use in the world, is eighth in gun deaths, twenty-fifth in alcohol consumption, in the top ten of countries with alcohol-related disorders—and in a new category, technological addiction, ranks twentieth in the world. These statistics are more shocking when considering that America contains less than 5 percent of the world's population.

We're all hypnotized to believe that "we are as we are," and "life is as it is," and nothing can change about either. Afterward, we believe: If we've been good, we'll go to heaven; if we were bad, we go to hell. To compare this worldview to the one Gurdjieff presents in *Beelzebub's Tales* is like living in the corner of the darkened basement of a huge mansion, not knowing there's a house above us. (This is the premise of Plato's Cave.)

Beelzebub tells us that the way upstairs begins by bringing that particle of the Divine into daily life. In other words, to begin to act from our conscience. When we make that conscious effort, a light switch is momentarily turned on, and we get a glimpse of another way to live with other possibilities.

CHAPTER THIRTY-FOUR

RUSSIA

THE being Beelzebub meets in Egypt has a wish to help his fellow countrymen, yet the foundation to eradicate alcoholism that he started was infiltrated by professional physicians, power-posing beings, and learned beings of New Format all with their own agendas. Because they were the ones "greasing the wheels," they became the foundation's decision makers. When they discovered that the ideas being implemented, which had been having a positive effect, came from someone who was not a member of one of their special clubs, there were immediate murmurings against these suggestions.

I felt that kind of prejudice once in high school. The students had to go outside into what at that time was a rough neighborhood in order to call someone for a pickup after a dance. All throughout junior and senior year I tried to get the school administration to have a public phone installed in the gymnasium's vestibule. In response, the administration conferred on me the title of rabble rouser, and my requests were derided, denied, and dismissed. Then, shortly after I graduated, three payphones were installed in the gym vestibule.

I'm sure Beelzebub's experience trying to get a permit is also familiar to anyone who needed to get something from a bureaucracy like a phone company or an insurance agency or the DMV. Self-importance and incompetence pervade these and other institutions that require soul-numbing work of their employees, who've had their hearts trained out of them.

Meeting the Czar is a perfect example of this type of training. Anyone who's met someone "of importance" or someone who is thought to be, understands the internal tribulations of such a meeting when the slightest misspoke word could cause a major incident. That's one of the reasons why celebrities and political candidates sound and act like puppets—they are.

On the other side are the "fans" who lose themselves at the sight of a famous person. It always begs the question—what makes someone important in our opinion? And the answer is usually the same. Though they may not have any detectable individual power, such as what comes from the struggle to create higher-being bodies, they are powerful in that they have sufficient means at their disposal to make the circumstances of one's life better or more miserable.

* * *

We're always sending vibrations out and receiving them back from people and things around us. Interestingly, we only notice this if they evoke an extraordinary response or sensation in us like when "out of the blue" we get a phone call from someone we've been thinking about. Scientists studying the invisible connections between people have verified that communicating thoughts and ideas by a means other than the known senses is possible, because, by design, we're all vibrationally connected.

We have receptors for cosmic influences as well, some of which come to us as laws like: gravity, breathing, eating, sleeping, and others of which we are unaware. If we can see the large number of influences we're under, we have a chance to free ourselves from some of them. One of the laws we can begin to look at Beelzebub calls Solioonensius, which is caused by a cyclical cosmic event. As celestial bodies approach being close to one another, their forces of attraction begin to affect each other, and they must strain to stay in their orbits, which strains the surrounding planets in their orbits.

We're familiar with this sensation, it's like when a stranger passes to close to us on the street. We feel the same kind of agitation because of the proximity of someone we don't know. As it's said, they're invading our personal space. We tense up, nerves on edge. Will they bother us? Cause us harm? You can feel the tension.

Celestial bodies feel the tension too. However, because of the difference in scale, what they feel as a passing moment we feel for months, and sometimes for years on the earth. We usually sense this planetary tension as nervous energy, which has two different effects on us. In the lower nature it feeds the tendency to anger, violence, crime, civil unrest, riots, and war. For a man or a woman striving to raise their level of being, that cosmic tension can energize one's aim, because it also evokes

> the feeling of religiousness, namely that 'being-feeling' which at times appears in the desire and striving for . . . speedier self-perfecting in the sense of Objective reason. (BT, 623)

It's not difficult to sense that the world's present state of agitation has a cosmic aspect to it, because human beings have no power over the outcome of these processes. For all the wishing in the world, we can do nothing on our level to change cosmic events. Some of the effects Solioonensius has on our planet are: virulent patriotism verging on fanaticism; religious zealotry; self-righteous extremism; widespread bigotry; and the systemic persecution of various segments of the population—resulting in explosive outbursts of violent revolution.

So how can knowing the effects of this law be useful? First, verify the idea for yourself. Are you agitated all the time, getting mad at the slightest provocation—generally pissed off? Are you quicker to argue and fight more often? Now look at the world: Do the same feelings seem to be coming from everyone? That's a sign of a cosmic influence, which makes it less personal, loosening its grip on you. That means that when you experience the negative effects, you can choose not to go with them, and instead you can practice taking in their influence positively.

Some laws, like gravity, we can't get by. But some we can get around; at least we don't have to pay their energy tax.

CHAPTER THIRTY-FIVE

A CHANGE *in the* APPOINTED COURSE *of* the TRANSSPACE SHIP KARNAK

THE most striking note in this chapter for me is Beelzebub's relationship to passing time. He's traveling to a celestial conference he's been asked to attend, and the thing I don't hear in his tone is rushing. If I put myself in his place, I'm immediately under a time constraint. When is the conference's scheduled start time? How long is the trip? Are we already late because we delayed for that cloud of Zilnotrago? Is there time to make another stop and visit someone?

It's interesting that no one but me seems to be concerned with passing time. Beelzebub is focused on making every minute count, including going to pay his respects to someone as dear and important to him as a parent. It raises the question of what do I focus my energy on in the course of my life, and what other possibilities are there?

CHAPTER THIRTY-SIX

JUST *a* WEE BIT MORE ABOUT *the* GERMANS

THANK God I'm not German, right? Wrong. German, French, American, Russian, Asian, and all the other cultures Beelzebub mentions represent different features in us. It's up to us to find those traits in ourselves so we can apply Gurdjieff's remedy to overcome them. For instance, the "grammatical rule" of German speech, putting a negation after an affirmation has become a fad today. You even hear it in scripted dialogue: "I love you—not!" As Beelzebub explains, psychologically, this initially gives the hearer a positive feeling, which is then quickly and cruelly snatched away. Among other things, this way of speaking dissolves all trust in the other person, because one is always waiting for the other shoe to drop.

There is also a more subtle form of this peculiarity, agreeing externally to do something while completely disagreeing with it on the inside. There's an outer affirmation, and an inner negation, so nothing ever happens. This seems to have morphed into another of today's fads—ghosting or never answering a particular question, and then disappearing either temporarily or permanently from the questioner's life. This is an extreme form of cowardice—never respond, never commit—a habit acquired in the computer world and applied to real life.

* * *

One interpretation of the poem is:

> Rubbish, rubbish is my amusement
> Dullness, dullness is my pleasure

CHAPTER THIRTY-SEVEN

FRANCE

THIS chapter is a funny and poignant look at the results of suggestibility. Beelzebub is taken on the Grand Duke's Tour to visit all the disreputable places in the city of Paris that he's heard so much about. Yet he sees that the people providing those entertainments and services are all foreigners. Think about your own preconceived notions of other nationalities and races. Can you look at someone from those "categories" of people and see the actual person in front of you? Further still, can you see them as a fellow creation under the same laws and influences as you, and having an equally difficult struggle with them in their life? Not without a conscious effort. We are more deeply hypnotized by life than we realize.

This pernicious trait is followed through the comical antics of the dance teacher, the seven cities in seven days tour company, and the real shark, that American exporter, showing that the beings breeding on the planet Earth are satisfied with the imagination of things, as long as it raises them in the estimation of others. The basis of the fashion industry is people's belief that altering their clothing changes their level of being. This goes for all of the ways there are to feel this way: the cars we drive, the technology we own, the jewelry we wear, the job we have, our significant other or lack of one, and the family we have or don't have.

In reality, these and many other of our daily practices are like vices we indulge in, in the hope of attaining:

To-a-complete-absence-of-the-need-for-being-effort-

and-for-every-essence-anxiety-of-whatever-kind-it-may-be. (BT, 688)

Our ultimate goal in life seems to be retiring with enough money to do nothing if we want. Whether we travel the world, build or buy the thing we've always wanted, or do whatever we've been wishing to accomplish in life "after we finish working," we want our surroundings to be pleasant, easy, and peaceful—meaning no internal upsets. This is the aim of our evil inner god of self-calming, which whenever real impulses arise in our being, invites us to use alcohol, drugs, sex, work, food, kids, sports, TV, the internet, or any other distraction so that we don't have to feel our inner life. Instead, we pass the time as pleasantly as possible as if there's time to pass. Think about the poem from the last chapter.

* * *

Ouspensky wrote a wonderful little book called *Talks with a Devil* in which the devil reveals different sides of himself than the ones we typically expect. One story explains how the devil really loves mankind, which is why he's continuously trying to make life easy for us. For instance, if after a big meal we might think of going for a walk to help our digestion, the Devil, not wanting us to exert ourselves, will rush over and fluff up the pillows on our couch.

* * *

Through the lens of these woke times one can see numerous landmines in this chapter that if approached the wrong way, can kill one's interest in perusing *Beelzebub's Tales*. Before we're sure, and get in a huff, we might give Gurdjieff the benefit of the doubt here and see if there's any truth to the rumor. Regarding the subject of women cutting their hair, these sentiments as well as their societal implications will appear blatantly misogynist until we can grasp the perspective Beelzebub is speaking from.

Women embody second force, or the holy receptive force, from which all things are created. Women have different parts then men, which are tuned to different frequencies. These must be in a certain proportion, so that all necessary vibrations are received. Cutting the hair short diminishes a woman's ability to receive certain cosmic influences, which is similar to a man with no facial hair. Anecdotally, I recently rewatched the original "Riverdance" show and noticed all the female dancers had long hair, which somehow psychologically added to their presence on stage in the context of the show.

Like everything else in Beelzebub's Tales, women and men are representative of influences, features, and forces. The truth of this idea must be proved or disproved to one's own satisfaction. The first step is to consider the emanations, radiations, and influences we unknowingly, sometimes ungratefully, receive from the surrounding cosmos. Which organ of perception are we taking them in with?

CHAPTER THIRTY-EIGHT

RELIGION

WHICH makes more sense, different Gods vying for control over the greater portion of Earth's population, or a Unified Endless Being sending various Messengers to different places on the planet so that—according to the people's heredity, geography, and social customs—they can begin to free themselves from the consequences of the organ Kundabuffer in order that they might consciously fulfill His Endlessness' hope for helpmates?

It's disturbing to realize that not one of the Messengers sent here from Above came to start a religion: Those are all man-made. They came into being because after the death of a Messenger their disciples collected the bits and pieces of their teachings that they remembered and wrote them down. After that, there were years and often centuries of tweaking, tinkering, clarifying, and interpreting—which always includes the requirements of the power-possessing beings and the needs of the professional clergy.

Is this too cynical a view? Not when we consider the fathers of the church, those philosophical clerics that interpretated real ideas without having made real-being efforts. This was how the Christ's teaching of love turned into the inquisition of nonbelievers. These "interpretations" became the various programs singling out women as witches, resulting in the torture and murder of over a million women healers, herbalists, and midwives during the Middle Ages. Also, as the Church's power and influence spread across Europe, leadership roles for women in the Church and society began disappearing. Women were systematically excluded from positions of authority, and all written accounts of powerful women were suppressed or erased. The Church went so far as to declare it heretical for anyone to advocate for women as priests.

Likewise, the genocide of Native Americans can be traced directly to these church fathers who declared other religions devil worship, granting their followers the right to purge them from the world. These doctrines continue today among religious fanatics striving to convert the world to their faith or kill it in the attempt.

Organized religion at heart is antithetical to inner evolution, which cannot be restrained by doctrine and dogma. This is not to say that there's nothing good or true in religious teachings. They all have some direct quotes from a Messenger, regarding right living and spiritual growth. Yet from a historical global perspective, organized religions have done and continue to do as much harm as good.

* * *

Regarding the universal view of Judas Iscariot as a heinous back-stabber, *National Geographic* published an article entitled "The Gospel of Judas" in May 2006. They reported that an "ancient text lost for 1,700 years" confirmed, "Christ's betrayer was his truest disciple." However, if we believe that Judas deceived and then betrayed Christ, we not only disparage Jesus's closest friend and ally, we cast doubt on Christ's Divinity. After all, how could a mortal mislead the Divine?

Likewise, when I typed into my search engine, "Why was the last supper held?" there were almost twenty million responses. The first number I read were "best guesses," and "hoped for" reasons to support one doctrine or another regarding the celebration of the Eucharist, like the following quote from the *Encyclopedia Britannica*:

> The letters of St. Paul the Apostle and the Acts of the Apostles demonstrate that early Christians believed that this institution [the Eucharist] included a mandate to continue the celebration as an anticipation in this life of

the joys of the banquet that was to come in the kingdom of God.

In other words, this Christian doctrine is not based on what Christ taught, but what his followers believed he intended, hoping for it to be true. In the Bible it says that Jesus sat down to Passover dinner with his Apostles. At one point He broke bread, said it was His body, and then offered his cup for all to drink from, saying,

> this cup is the new testament *in my blood* [my italics], which is shed for you. (Luke 22:20, KJV)

It sounds as though Christ has just shed his blood and filled the cup with it. This becomes a real possibility if the above quote is coupled with one from the gospel of John:

> Then Jesus said unto them, Verily, verily, I say unto you, Except ye eat the flesh of the Son of Man, and drink His blood, ye have no life in you. (John 6:53, KJV)

Jesus lost a number of disciples when he spoke those words because they were considered too harsh to follow. Christ even asked His Apostles if they were also going to leave Him because of what he'd taught. These quotes bring the popular grasp of the Lord's Supper and the traditional understanding of "celebrating" mass into question, which of course is Gurdjieff's intention.

As a side note, the traditional Native American practice of blood brotherhood has many echoes in what Gurdjieff is explaining about invisible bonds between people sharing blood.

CHAPTER THIRTY-NINE

THE HOLY PLANET "PURGATORY"

THIS chapter is a God's-eye-view of the universe, and the heart of the book. It's the "why" of creation. Beelzebub explains that the Megalocosmos came into existence because the dwelling place of His Endlessness was shrinking over time, as everything was proceeding out from the Protocosmos. His Endlessness came to understand that His system had to be changed to a system where energy would continue to go out but also some would return to His dwelling place to stop the shrinkage. To correct the situation, He altered the two fundamental cosmic laws of the universe, creating a system of reciprocal feeding.

* * *

His Endlessness sent out the Theomertmalogus (Word of God, Will of the Absolute) to begin creation, which then proceeded mechanically through Divine laws. In the course of their involution and evolution the universe slowly expanded. Due to these same processes beginning on the planet Earth, there eventually arose one-, two-, and three-brained beings. When His Endlessness saw these creations, He believed that the three-brained human beings, under certain circumstances (i.e., the coating of higher-being bodies) could be useful in the administration of the expanding universe. Those beings are us. We've been given the possibility of fulfilling this hope in the performance of our assigned task of supporting Earth and its moons.

We were designed as transforming apparatuses of cosmic influences to assist with feeding the Earth and the moon. Yet we've also been given the possibility of doing so consciously, and thereby transforming some of the influences we ingest into higher and finer energies for our inner evolution. The process of transformation of daily bread into higher-being bodies requires conscious labor and intentional suffering, which is not necessarily what we think it is. For instance, sacrificing our favorite way of thinking or feeling or doing to achieve an aim is intentionally suffering. (A detailed explanation of the transformation of the three being foods can be found in Chapter 9 of P. D. Ouspensky's book *In Search of the Miraculous*.)

* * *

This chapter is an astoundingly complete and detailed account of creation, including the big bang theory. Although I cannot imagine what initiating the Theomertmalogus equals in terms of megatons of explosive creative power. After that initial burst of Divine Will, the sacred laws of creation and manifestation took over, and the world as we know it slowly sprang into being from the all-universal substance filling space, the result of the initial creative impulse of Divine separation. Is there a simpler, more common-sense scenario that explains the "how" and "why" of creation and the necessity of world maintenance?

* * *

Purgatory in Roman Catholic doctrine is a place of suffering for souls who've been given the opportunity to expiate their sins and thereby possibly gain entrance into heaven. Though this sounds remarkably close to what Beelzebub describes, its perspective is an exceedingly low one. What do we think we do in Purgatory? How does our sin get expiated? This says a lot about how we think of heaven, and how easy or difficult we believe it is to enter. Beelzebub tells Hassein it's almost impossible for beings from Earth to achieve this now. Thankfully, our salvation lies in the word *almost*, which means it's not impossible. The place to start is by thinking of oneself as a vessel for a drop of Divinity, with the possibility of becoming a cell in the head-brain of our Endless Uni-Being Creator. This will organize our thoughts, feelings, and actions in the right order.

*   *   *

Our ideas of heaven and hell usually come from a very low perspective in us. Heaven is a place of indescribable happiness and peace where every earthly pleasure, from rivers of milk and honey to having nubile virgins at your beck and call 24/7/365. All we have to do is sing a few praises of the Lord now and again. Hell is a place of endless physical pain and suffering, to which we'll go if we've been really bad.

From Beelzebub's perspective, heaven is being useful to our Endlessness in helping to fulfill His most sacred aim. Hell is being separated from and useless to our Uni-being Creator.

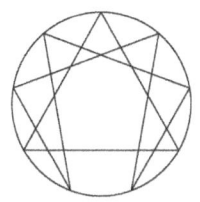

BOOK THREE

CHAPTER FORTY

BEELZEBUB TELLS HOW PEOPLE LEARNED *and* FORGOT ABOUT *the* FUNDAMENTAL COSMIC LAW *of* HEPTAPARAPARSHINOKH

I am not going to address any of the particularities of the two fundamental cosmic laws or the various sciences and apparatuses discussed. That is a much broader topic than the scope of this present work. Instead, I'm compelled to relate the old Sufi tale of the novitiate's dream.

A young monk had a strange dream one night, and the next morning he went to his abbot for an explanation. He told him that in his dream he was standing on the shore of a great ocean next to a very old monk of their order. Suddenly, the old monk leaped off the beach and flew gracefully over the water, landing gently on the other shore. Sometime later, another monk came up to him on the beach, and he too leaped out over the water. His flight was much lower, and sometimes he'd skim the water and splash along the surface, struggling to get back into the air. Finally, he also made it across, though he landed a bit less gracefully then the first monk. Then a third monk stood next to him. He also leaped up, and immediately fell into the water. He had to swim practically all the way, and was half drowned a number of times before he, too, finally got across and crawled out onto the other shore.

The abbot explained that it was a dream about the ages. The first monk's journey was at a time long ago when the circumstances for becoming a sacred individual were much more favorable, and inner development was more natural. Then the conditions on Earth worsened, and the second monk's flight was proportionately more difficult. By the time the third monk arrived, circumstances had deteriorated to a point where sustained flight was out of the question. The novitiate nodded solemnly to express his understanding, and then the abbot asked him which monk's journey he thought was more highly prized by our Endless Creator.

It's true that in our time it's objectively more difficult to evolve. This is partly because we're coming simultaneously to the end of a number of cosmic octaves that will all require extra efforts by mankind to continue on. And this is possible. We were born with the germ of objective reason in us as well as a drop of the Divine in the form of our conscience. The rest is up to us. Like attracts like. Through our conscious labors and intentional sufferings, we can coat energy-particles within us that eventually form higher-being bodies. This is the promise of salvation at the root of all religions.

* * *

One of our conscious labors must be to acquire knowledge of the laws of manifestation and creation—the "how" and "why" of coating higher-being bodies. Also, we must develop the potency to be sincere with ourselves and learn how not to be overtaken by externals, especially our inherent passions. Intentional suffering comes from a wish to be useful, and understanding that we aren't.

CHAPTER FORTY-ONE

THE BOKHARIAN DERVISH HADJI-ASVATZ-TROOV

Carnivorous animal attacks on people around the world have been steadily increasing since 1950.[19] In this light, Beelzebub's idea that predatory animal's sensing human fear as a danger makes sense. As he says, these animals

> perceive the inner feeling of fear in other beings before them as enmity towards themselves and therefore strive to destroy these others in order to avert the "menace" from themselves. (BT, 877)

We fear animals because we don't know them. Somehow they're below our radar, so when one pops up, we're frightened, and—like the "war hero"—when our feelings of self-perseveration kick in, we become violent. Contrast this to stories about Daniel in the lion's den, and Saint Francis of Assisi.

The British artist, Briton Rivière, known for his realistic wildlife paintings captured the story of Daniel in his painting titled, *"Daniel's Answer to the King."* Daniel is shown gazing up at the sun, which is spilling in through a high window in his cell while all the lions are keeping a respectful distance and staring at him in wonder, knowing he's a different kind of being. When asked why God saved him, Daniel said, "because I was found blameless."[20] Blameless for what? He is speaking from the *I* in him, that part of him which is Divine— that which is truly blameless. The lions sense his higher being and are in awe.

St. Francis of Assisi discovered "something not quite right" in himself, and through his efforts to purge it from his being became one with all the Earth's creatures. He was said to be able to preach to the birds and tame wild wolves. Are these stories simply biblical morality tales, or as Beelzebub says, are they the "piece here and a piece there" of the knowledge of objective being?

* * *

The Dervish Hadji-Asvatz-Troov is an illustration of the old esoteric saying: Following a question all the way to the end will lead one to the Divine. All his experimental apparatuses as well as all the amenities of his cave came from his quest. He's achieved a level of being high enough where Beelzebub is allowed to be frank with him and reveal his true nature. If you're wondering why Beelzebub is not allowed to discuss real ideas with those of insufficient being, think of the times on Earth that flashes of so-called inspiration turned into weapons of mass destruction.

CHAPTER FORTY-TWO

BEELZEBUB in AMERICA

BEELZEBUB is holding up a mirror to American sensibilities, now emulated globally, and it's not pretty. We're obsessed with money or, as Beelzebub calls it, dollar business. The center of American government is not in Washington, it's in the stock market. In 1925 then-President Calvin Coolidge said,

> the chief business of the American people is business. They are profoundly concerned with producing, buying, selling, investing, and prospering in the world.[21]

This has led to America being more of a going concern then a country, and its citizens—merely wallets and purses to be plundered. Advertisements, movies, video broadcasts, radio shows, podcasts, news outlets, and all the rest try to sell us something, be it a product or a viewpoint. Their sales pitches are typically filled with titillation and put forth at a fever pitch as though our lives depended on it. Sex and fear are tremendous selling points.

The more we chase after products that supposedly save us time and money and have others doing our physical chores for us, the less we're able to do for ourselves. This is especially true for the construction trades, restaurants, agricultural industry, child care, elder care, and other services that wouldn't exist without immigrants filling their labor force. In 2004 an insightful, though not well received, satirical movie debuted on the topic called *A Day Without a Mexican*. It showed the people of California struggling to meet the demands of life without the help of migrant workers. Needless to say, they couldn't manage it.

* * *

We're addicted to comfort. We want an easy life, everything done for us with as little effort on our part as possible. Of course, there are those who can't stop working, but that is their comfort. Food, clothing, and entertainment can be delivered to our doors—we don't have to move from our house. The expression "there's an App for that," has become ubiquitous in our time.

Interestingly, I found an article about a bed that was recently unveiled with added features like surround sound speakers, a movie projector, internet connectivity, a phone docking port, and dual temperature controls. So, how far are we from having refrigerators, air fryers, and toilet facilities in our comfy couches?

* * *

What does wartime chicken soup and prohibition have in common? Suggestibility, for one thing. Prohibition was known as "the Noble Experiment," and for over a decade:

> The law that was meant to foster temperance instead fostered intemperance and excess.... It is very clear that in many parts of the United States more people were drinking, and people were drinking more ... [Also] on average, 1000 Americans died every year during the prohibition from the effects of drinking tainted liquor.[22]

Likewise, the incantation for chicken soup by that famous Professor is the equivalent of the German government's propaganda machine during both world wars that told its citizens they should be honored to starve for the Fatherland—and they believed it. Or the British government during WW II telling its people to ignore all the destruction and death around them—and just "carry on," which they did.

* * *

In our world of duality there are meat eaters and vegetarians. Both of these are intellectual positions or decisions of taste that come from limited knowledge and personal feeling. We look only at the face of things and leave out their higher purposes. This comes from thinking we know what things are, and we know how best to deal with them. Objective science takes into account the physical, psychic, and cosmic properties of a substance before determining its usefulness as food.

Hertoonano, "the greatest authority on the laws of the inner organization of man" (BT, 1016), understood the idea of digestion and the refinement of higher energies. From his study we have the idea of fasting from certain cosmic substances during certain times of the year because of how these foods affect us psychically and physically. This is the epitome of common sense. However, our lack of understanding, or any wish to want to understand, gets us into food fights about who should eat what. It's said, "a little knowledge is dangerous," but a little understanding can go a long way.

* * *

Beelzebub takes on English as it's spoken in America, and he's spot on in terms of every generation wanting to separate itself from the previous one and having its own language as part of the process. The language of texting which has now crept into "formal" writing is a perfect example. Unless you are part of that generation, it's work to decipher their references. The problem is that this only serves to further separate people into smaller groups who might soon lose the ability to communicate with each other all together.

* * *

Beelzebub says that America will eventually die of infrasex and indigestion. (Infrasex is pleasuring the planetary body solely for its own sake.) Now, almost a hundred years later, we can grasp for ourselves the blossoms of this prediction.

Our food today is of very low quality in terms of possessing useful substances for our digestion. It's manipulated and processed from start to finish and is mostly filler, providing little nutritional benefit for all of our different brains. In America today, 60 million people have chronic constipation,[23] and in 2004, 20 percent of America's population had Gastroesophageal Reflux Disease.[24] Needless to say, these numbers are increasing yearly.

Regarding infrasex, there is a disheartening trend among young girls to turn to the pornography industry or the sex trade for their livelihood. This, of course, is not disconnected from the movies glorifying the industry and showing young, impressionable girls the benefits of "owning their own bodies." This real idea was warped into meaning that they can abuse themselves however they want; it's for them to decide. This is only reinforced by the costumes various celebrities and influencers wear to public events. Dressing this way creates a constant state of titillation, which devours our psychic energy while furthering the loss of organic shame in our beings.

> Forty million Americans regularly visit porn sites, and 35 percent of all internet downloads are related to pornography.[25]

This is particularly harmful to the young—as,

> among adolescents . . . pornography hinders the development of healthy sexuality, and distorts sexual attitudes and social realities.[26]

* * *

People today seem to either zealously believe in some fixed idea, or believe in nothing. In other words, we're in a world of duality where there's only dogma or disbelief. This is especially true today in America where the country is split almost evenly down the middle on every issue, and no one is willing to compromise.

Can we hold advertising responsible for this situation? Yes, I believe so. It has been a slow process but an inevitable one. What percentage of marketing claims do you believe? How many times has a product been disappointing. For instance, has that beautifully advertised hamburger ever arrived in your take-out bag? This leads to disbelief in what anyone says. If we understood the insidious effect this disbelief has on our psyches, we'd never again give our attention to another advertisement for a product, religious stance, candidate, proposal, etc.—without a large grain of salt.

*   *   *

One of the connections Beelzebub draws is between stifling our feelings of remorse of conscience and physical disease. It's not a big stretch to imagine that a blockage in the digestion of emotions would impact other systems. It's in the expression when one is emotionally distressed, "My stomach feels like it's tied in knots."

It's an interesting exercise to think about the recent Covid pandemic as the result of people acting against their convictions. The first question is, have I experienced going against conscience? Next, did it make me sick to my stomach?

CHAPTER FORTY-THREE

BEELZEBUB'S SURVEY *of the* PROCESS *of* the PERIODIC DESTRUCTION OF MEN, *or* BEELZEBUB'S OPINION OF WAR

OUR news today is so thoroughly controlled and manipulated that you wouldn't know there were many global antiwar movements unless you were part of them. Likewise, war deaths today are "only" in the hundreds of thousands, and usually out of sight and out of mind. In other words, we get the fear factor but no real facts. During the writing of *Beelzebub's Tales*, World War I had run its course, and WWII had also begun and finished. In the intervening twenty-five years an estimated 63 to 107 million people died as a direct result of man's propensity for reciprocal destruction. That was over 3 percent of the world's population at the time. Needless to say, Gurdjieff burned with the hope of finding some way to end this human atrocity and slap in Divinity's face.

* * *

Today we've become almost immune to tragedy because it comes at us so fast and there are so many of them. This is also true of the ecological crisis we're presently experiencing. From one point of view, the world is too large to think about its problems. How can I stop the huge mechanisms at work that continue the process of global warming? Interestingly, just in today's news, sixteen children ages five to twenty-two sued the state of Montana for not providing them with a clean environment—and won. If you believe you can do something—you can. If you don't believe, you won't be able to.

* * *

BEELZEBUB'S SURVEY *of the* PROCESS *of the* PERIODIC DESTRUCTION

One reason mankind continues carrying on with the process of reciprocal destruction is that people only consider the question of war when their bellies are full and their personal emotions are stirred. In other words, we don't think about anything else until our desires are satisfied and we feel an emotional connection to the topic. As Beelzebub said, common sense and seeing reality are luxuries today, a point Gurdjieff was making almost a hundred years ago, and the problem hasn't gotten better. Mankind is focused on its survival, though sadly not in a unified way. It's "every man for himself," each of us focused on our daily struggle to come out on top. The wealthy with satiated desires could do something about this terrible process of reciprocal destruction, but they either have no interest or are profiting from it—their biggest crime.

The devastating process of war also continues because of the lack of unified leadership in the world. All attempts to form a society against continuing the process of reciprocal destruction start off with a bang and end with a whimper. Even the 1960s anti-Vietnam-war movement faded away after a few key assassinations and a public execution on an American college campus.

Another factor in the continuation of this horrible process is thinking that thousands of years of habit can be changed in a few decades. This is working for the present, which most of us do. We want to change things now, for us. An indication of a higher level of consciousness is working for the future, making things better for those who will follow us. Beelzebub says that if war-hero worship is eliminated now, something that could be accomplished in a lifetime, wars would eventually end. This makes absolute sense, which is why there is a Military-Entertainment Complex to saturate American society in war-hero worship through the production of major motion pictures, music videos, and video games—as well as sponsoring NASCAR racing and most professional sporting events.

* * *

The aim of inner evolution is to be inner driven. That means intentionally taking in and digesting impressions and coating our inner selves in those energy particles—thereby creating an individual unified *I* that directs us in an upwardly spiraling direction. In part, this is accomplished by stopping dualistic thinking—this *or* that—and beginning to think in terms of this *and* that.

*   *   *

Beelzebub tells the story of how, long ago, a conference was held to determine why wars occur on Earth, with the aim of stopping them. The greatest learned being of the land attended, yet he had only a partial grasp of cosmic laws. His first conclusion was that the universe was based on the law of reciprocal feeding, which is an accurate understanding. Yet he erroneously believed that a higher quantity of the energy released at death was required at certain times of the year for higher cosmic purposes. That made war a necessary evil, which threw their antiwar conference into turmoil. Then this learned being came to his second conclusion: The required number of deaths did not have to be human. And so, once again the practice of animal sacrifice was initiated on the Earth.

Beelzebub laments that this great learned being was onto something, but he was missing certain cosmic details of what was needed—an increase in the quality of vibrations, not the quantity. During the time of Ashiata Shiemash, when humanity in that part of the world was giving off finer vibrations, not only did war end, but the death rate dropped, as well as the birth rate, because more people were living by their conscious reason, according to design.

*   *   *

The last part of this chapter is particularly offensive to our modern sensibilities. One reason for this is that we've come to have a tissue-thin skin. Even the hint of some idea or statement being offensive will bring down a torrent of negativity. The other reason is that we are not looking for understanding, but instead we believe without a single doubt that our interpretation of what is written on the page is the right one.

Beelzebub is looking at the situation from a much higher level—the necessary, cosmically determined support for the Earth and its moons, and the possibility of individuals growing higher-being bodies. So, the idea of three sexes and separating them at fixed times of the year is an examination of human psychology, not physicality. That's why he defines the third sex by those four being characteristics—not their choice of partners or lack thereof.

* * *

We are especially on guard today for any perceived insults or slights against who we believe we are. Part of the reason is that we don't know who we are, so we take particular care to construct acceptable versions of ourselves that we don't want challenged. We have to learn how to accurately measure ourselves and our true worth from the eye of the Divine, not our fellow man.

CHAPTER FORTY-FOUR

IN *the* OPINION *of* BEELZEBUB, MAN'S UNDERSTANDING *of* JUSTICE *is for* HIM *in the* OBJECTIVE SENSE *an* ACCURSED MIRAGE

It may be difficult to grasp the ideas in this chapter because our perspective is modern, and we fully accept the idea of good and evil coming to us from outside ourselves. It's the old joke—the devil made me do it. However, the evolutionary octave is also called "evil" because it goes against or opposite to the flow of life. (It's not a coincidence that live spelled backwards is evil.)

Active force *involves*—passive force *evolves*. This means that creation is a masculine process—evolution is a feminine process. A creative octave pushes into the world away from the One. An evolutionary octave seeks return and reunion with the One. Does this concur with your current concept of good and evil?

It's nonsensical to think that good and evil are external forces in the Megalocosmos, operating on us like an angel sitting on one shoulder, whispering good ideas to us while a tiny devil sits on the other, tempting us to do wrong. Those temptations are inside us from the part of us that doesn't want to work and is looking for an excuse not to.

Believing in good and evil outside ourselves feeds our inner god of self-calming by relieving us of responsibility for our actions. This way we can say things like "the spirit was willing, but the flesh was weak." From the perspective of individual evolution, that's a baseline—we know that. The question is: What will you do, knowing that. We have to make the spirit responsible for the flesh and, outside of accident and chance, direct our lives toward our aims and wishes. It's useful to remember that regarding the circumstances of our lives, we're more volunteer than victim.

CHAPTER FORTY-FIVE

IN the OPINION of BEELZEBUB, MAN'S EXTRACTION of ELECTRICITY from NATURE and ITS USE is ONE of the CHIEF CAUSES of the SHORTENING of the LIFE of MAN

THE dictionary defines *electricity* as a type of energy that results from the existence of charged particles such as electrons and protons, which are together either *statically* as an accumulation of charge (a battery) or *dynamically* as a current (a live wire). A charged particle is defined as a particle with an electric charge. So basically, science doesn't understand the force or charge called "electricity" or where it comes from.

Beelzebub explains that electricity is caused by extracting positive and negative forces from nature, and then re-blending them artificially without a third force present. Their striving to re-blend in abnormal conditions creates an electric charge (friction?), which we then use to power our lights, machines, electronics, cars, and all the other blessings we've created that run on electricity.

Everything is made up of energy-matter in certain ratios. From the tiniest to the greatest differences between things is only a matter of quality and quantity of vibrations. In other words, we're all made from the same material, only in different proportions, measured by the fineness or coarseness of our vibrations. The three forces in a planet's atmosphere are the original sources of those vibrations for that world, and as such must be maintained in a certain ratio in order for the processes of creation and maintenance on the planet Earth to continue.

The problem with making electricity is that it uses up two of the three creative forces. Needless to say, this throws our entire planetary system out of balance. This results in a cascading effect of degradation on all the following manifestations: An unbalanced atmosphere means that our air, water, and ground are out of balance (i.e., missing certain properties or vibrations). Under these poorer conditions the substances formed on Earth will also be poorer in quality. The higher substances that coat higher-being bodies may be missing from our foods and cease to exist all together. If electrical extraction continues unabated, spiritual evolution and life itself may eventually become impossible on planet Earth.

For the day-to-day, electrical overuse and waste accelerates the negative effects of climate change, resulting in higher global temperatures and increasing frequency of extreme weather events. Also, the resulting light pollution diminishes the view of the stars in the night sky, lowering the number of finer impressions available to us.

Although it's almost impossible to live without electricity these days, as anyone who's experienced a blackout can attest to, we must begin to understand the consequences of its criminal waste. A simple way to start is one your parents probably often said—turn the lights off when you leave a room. Also, when you're in the room, ask yourself if there's enough light with the sun in the windows, or must you turn on an electric light to see what you're doing? They're not big efforts, but they'll lead to an increase of consciousness.

Why do we need to see empty buildings lit up all through the night? Why isn't emergency lighting sufficient? Why do our roads and highways need to be lit up like high noon? Why can't our streetlamps and highway lights be designed to serve their purpose without illuminating everything for hundreds of yards around? At night, from space our planet looks like a lighting store's gaudy window display. Are all those lights necessary or useful? Is the loss of the materiality for creating a soul a price worth paying to see flashing electronic billboards 24/7?

CHAPTER FORTY-SIX

BEELZEBUB EXPLAINS to HIS GRANDSON the SIGNIFICANCE of the FORM and SEQUENCE WHICH HE CHOSE for EXPOUNDING the INFORMATION CONCERNING MAN

Beelzebub's glad that his grandson is crying, because having empathy for the beings on the Earth shows the development of the connection to his conscience. Conscience can be defined as feeling all together. We seldom know what anyone else is feeling; often, we barely know how we feel. Gurdjieff taught that a number-five man, someone on a high level of consciousness, feels the suffering of all of humanity. This trait was further developed by the being called Jesus Christ, who took all of man's suffering to the cross with Him as an offering for mankind's salvation.

* * *

Beelzebub has taken responsibility for Hassein's education, and he's laid out chapter-by-chapter the steps toward inner evolution. First, he explains to Hassein that he's made a conscious effort not to give him his own opinions but only verifiable facts, leaving his grandson to draw his own conclusions.

The stories Beelzebub told Hassein about the civilizations on Earth can be taken internally. *As above—so below* means that every cosmos is based on the same laws and principles and relies on the same being-functions. We are a Megalocosmos in miniature, and what's said to one applies to all; it's only a matter of degree.

In the same way, Hassein, Ahoon, and all the other beings,

including Beelzebub, that populate that world are also in our inner world. These lessons can be very profitable as long as we don't get indignant, offended, vexed, and so forth (BT, 1170).

Take the idea that there is a difference between the reason of knowledge and the reason of understanding. Although we often use the terms interchangeably, they are not. Understanding is the result of a conscious effort, where we take the knowledge we've acquired in life, verify it, and apply it to our being. Knowledge plus being equals understanding, which becomes an inseparable part of us that we can reason from. This reason can only grow in us by conscious effort and intentional suffering.

When we reason from acquired knowledge, our thinking is driven by information, which is prone to change. This means that with each new impression from outside, our position on an issue can alter. Even positions we're adamant about can drift to the wayside of our mind because knowledge is unconnected to our experience.

When we're given an intellectual fact from life it gets stored in the head brain. It's the same with emotional and moving facts, which get stored in their particular brains. The instinctive part of the moving brain is self-sufficient, and except for getting sick or being otherwise out of balance, it doesn't need our input. In fact, our input is usually the problem. Also, we gravitate toward the things we like—so, in people, one brain is always more developed than the other two. This is why intellectual types do intellectual things, emotional types do emotional things, etc. This makes us lopsided. Gurdjieff taught that one should exercise each of their brains daily. A complete number-four man can be thought of as a combination of Albert Einstein, Mother Teresa, and Michael Jordan.

CHAPTER FORTY-SEVEN

THE INEVITABLE RESULT of IMPARTIAL MENTATION

Many things in life give us guarantees. Sadly, most of these are disappointing when it comes time to collect on them. Gurdjieff makes no promises. He does say that if you work to digest the ideas he's presented, they'll work on you for your benefit. It's in the title of the chapter: The result of conscious labor and intentional suffering is an increase in consciousness, conscience, being, and usefulness.

The last thing he says in the context of the tales is that if we ponder our death in a positive way, we can live the life we were meant to live. If we don't, there's no chance. Death is the stroke that makes life real. Because we think that we'll never die, we believe we have all the time in the world to change.

CHAPTER FORTY-EIGHT

FROM *the* AUTHOR

The highest aim and sense of human life is the striving to attain the welfare of one's neighbor, and this is possible exclusively only by the conscious renunciation of one's own" (BT, 1186).

THIS is similar to Christ's teaching about turning the other cheek, a practically impossible idea to follow in daily life. "How can I possibly get anywhere in life if I always put others first?" That's not what Gurdjieff is saying. First there's scale—he's talking about the *highest* aim. And of course, if you're working for another's welfare, you can't put your own benefit first. When we look at ourselves framed by Divinity's needs, then "getting somewhere" becomes a different question. Also, it's not a matter of putting others first to your own detriment, it's working for their betterment. And the place to start is correcting one's own flaws first.

END NOTES

1) G. I. Gurdjieff, *Life is Real Only Then, When "I Am," All and Everything/Third Series* (New York: Triangle/Doubleday & McClure, 1975), 26, 271.

2) American Psychological Association, "Forgiveness: A Sampling of Research Results," (Washington, DC: Office of International Affairs, 2006, reprinted 2008).

3) Holy Bible, King James Version, Romans, 7:19.

4) P. D. Ouspensky, *In Search of the Miraculous: Fragments of an Unknown Teaching* (New York: Harcourt, Brace & World, 1949), 332/Table 8.

5) John Milton, *Paradise Lost: An Authoritative Text, Backgrounds and Sources, Criticism*, ed. Scott Elledge (New York: W.W. Norton, 1975), line 263.

6) Gurdjieff, *Life is Real Only Then, When "I Am,"* 246.

7) Holy Bible, King James Version, Genesis 1.

8) Avi Selk, *Washington Post* (Yahoo news, AFP article, October 21, 2017).

9) Ibid.

10) Holy Bible, King James Version, Matthew 7:7–8.

11) Jeffrey Kluger, "Earth Has a Second Moon—For Another 300 Years, At Least," *Time* online magazine, November 11, 2021.

12) Holy Bible, King James Version, Genesis, 1:1.

13) Rodney Collin, *The Theory of Celestial Influence: Man, the Universe and Cosmic Mystery* (Boulder, CO: Shambhala, 1984), 2.

14) Salih Muhammad Awadh, PhD, "Solar system planetary alignment triggers tides and earthquakes, *Journal of Coastal Conservation* 25, no. 30 (March 2021).

15) Amira Shamma Abdin, "Love in Islam," *European Judaism: A Journal for the New Europe* 37, no. 1 (Spring 2004): 92–102.

16) *The Mystery of the Sphinx*, (based on *Serpent in the Sky* by John Anthony West), award-winning documentary, directed and written by Bill Cote, featuring narrator Charlton Heston, aired November 10, 1993, on NBC and subsequently over 10 years on TLC and the Discovery Channel.

17) "Internet Pornography by the Numbers; A Significant Threat to Society," webroot.com.

18) Kathy Reeves, "Whatever Happened to Roy G Biv?" *Our Favorite Scientific Minds Are Those We Teach* (blog), *Scientific Minds*, September 14, 2016.

19) Nidhi Sharma, "Carnivores' attacks on humans are becoming more common, and climate change isn't helping," NBC News, February 7, 2023.

20) Holy Bible, King James Version, Daniel 6:22.

21) Calvin Coolidge, "The Press Under a Free Government," address to the American Society of Newspaper Editors on the rights and privileges that come with journalism and writing under a free government. Washington, DC: January 17, 1925.

22) Michael Lerner, "Unintended Consequences of Prohibition," online article promoting three-part video documentary *Prohibition* by Ken Burns and Lynn Novick, produced by PBS Documentaries, https://www.pbs.org/kenburns/prohibition/unintended-consequences.

23) P. D. Higgins and J. F. Johanson, "Epidemiology of Constipation in *North America*," *American Journal of Gastroenterology* 99, no. 4 (April 2004):750–59.

24) Hashem B. El-Serag, Nancy J. Petersen, Junaia Carter, et al. "Gastroesophageal reflux among different racial groups in the United States," *Gastroenterology AGA* 126, no. 7 (June 2004): 1692–99.

25) "Internet pornography by the Numbers," webroot.com.

26) Ibid.

STEPHEN BURZI was born, raised, and schooled in New York City, graduating with a Bachelor of Arts in English Literature, which he studied because "literature tells the truth about history." Since graduation—alongside a continuing study of various religions, mythologies, philosophies, cosmologies, and G. I. Gurdjieff's opus, *Beelzebub's Tales to His Grandson*—he has enjoyed a long, successful, and fulfilling career supervising large-scale commercial construction projects in the New York Tristate area.

www.ingramcontent.com/pod-product-compliance
Lightning Source LLC
Chambersburg PA
CBHW022006100426
42738CB00041B/684